Go and Do Likewise:
Following Jesus into our Common Humanity

Terry B. Kyllo

Cover Art
Cover: Healing Hummingbird © Jay Bowen 2023
http://jaybowen-art.com/wordpress/

Cover Design
Shelby Kyllo

Download Discussion Questions, Action Steps, & Resources:
https://pathstounderstanding.org/gdl/

Praise for Go and Do Likewise

Terry's wonderful book is written about a topic I have been focused on for all of my teaching career. Coming from an ordained Lutheran pastor gives his interpretation of religious pluralism more currency than is possible in a university classroom setting. I can hardly wait for its publication so I can add it to my own library. But more importantly, his interpretation of religious pluralism needs to be part of the religious education curriculum of local church communities.
   Paul O. Ingram, Professor Emeritus, Pacific Lutheran University

This book helps us to better understand the beauty of Christianity and explains how it has been misused to rationalize hatred and dehumanization of others. Rev. Kyllo teaches us to use our wisdom traditions to honor one another and to help create meaningful relationships with others. It is a powerful message.
   Rabbi Allison Flash

This remarkable book is filled with wisdom and hope. The author beautifully models the precious truth that to love Jesus is to make a commitment to tame the ego and open the heart, to celebrate God's diversity on earth, and to be of humble service to all of Creation.
   Imam Jamal Rahman, author of Spiritual Gems of Islam

Rev. Kyllo's book "Go and Do Likewise" is a must-read for all those who wish to reverse the recent uptick in racial and religious bigotry which has led to physical and emotional assaults on the most vulnerable in our society. The only thing that enables evil to thrive is when good people are silent. Read this book and give it as a holiday or birthday gift. We all will be safer if you do.
   Rabbi James Mirel
   Seattle WA

Terry Kyllo's new book Go and Do Likewise: Following Jesus into our Common Humanity examines how Christianity can get off course and back on course by investigating deeply the sources of the Abrahamic tradition. Fear tends to divert the core teaching of Jesus and other wisdom traditions around the world into insular in-groups who often protect themselves by vilifying and dehumanizing others. We all know deep down that love diminishes the artificial barriers between ourselves and others, where we can more easily work for the common good of all beings on this vibrant planet. This book works to restate and recover the many ways that the Abrahamic tradition, and more specifically the Christian tradition, is called to relate and partner with diverse traditions and peoples. Rev. Kyllo is not interested in labels like "conservative" or "liberal." He is very interested in a humble and honest investigation of the Bible by better understanding the cultural, historical, and linguistic context in which the verses were written. This book strives to have a faithful-and-open-to-revision understanding of Jesus' ministry and how it applies today. It is my joy to highly recommend this book to any person of faith who is willing to actively work for more harmony and understanding in our troubled world.

Rev. Genjo Marinello, Abbot. Seattle Zen Temple
Dai Bai Zan Cho Bo Zen Ji

As we pursue justice in this balkanized world, we desperately need coconspirators to create a more just and humane world. In this work Terry Kyllo points us in the direction of collaboration rooted in the teaching and life of Jesus. As we engage faithful community-building behaviors this work is an important contribution to building the infrastructure of trust necessary to form healthy coalitions.

Rt. Rev. Edward Donalson III, DMin | Provost Fellow for Ecumenical Relations SCHOOL OF THEOLOGY AND MINISTRY | SEATTLE UNIVERSITY

Three Great Teachings of the Abrahamic Tradition Adapted for This Moment

Love God more than your
in-group and tradition

Love your neighbor
as you love yourself

Steward a thriving ecosystem and
an equitable economy

Table of Contents

Download Discussion Questions, Action Steps, & Resources:
https://pathstounderstanding.org/gdl/

Introduction and Acknowledgements

This book is the result of many conversations with the tradition of Jesus, scholars of the Christian and Hebrew traditions, Christian communities seeking a more faithful way to follow Jesus, and leaders of many wisdom traditions. I have spoken to hundreds of leaders about what is leading to a loss of social trust in the United States and what we can do about it.

Over time, I realized that each tradition brings an analysis of the positive and negative potentials of humans and human communities. I began to ask leaders to analyze our current situation and what strategies can bring out our best. Each tradition brings different gifts and perspectives. Yet I found that our traditions hold much wisdom in common.

Some shared analyses: We are lonely and isolated, we are divided into exclusive in-groups, and we are dehumanizing each other.

Some shared strategies: We grow in trust when we know each other, work for the common good together, and honor each other in public spaces.

I believe that the Abrahamic tradition, like many wisdom traditions around the world, began in response to exclusive in-grouping and dehumanization, leading to injustice and violence.

This book is an attempt to restate and recover the many ways the Abrahamic tradition, generally, and the Christian tradition, specifically, calls participants to honor, relate to, and partner with diverse in-groups and traditions. The intent of the book and the online course is to help Christians find our "why" for honoring, relating to, and partnering with people of other traditions.

As a cradle Christian, I was taught just the opposite: I was taught that, in Christianity, God calls forth an exclusive in-group that can and should use dehumanizing language against other communities of wisdom until they convert. Under this, of course, I felt the threat that I would be outcast from the Christian community and rejected by God if I behaved or believed differently.

Over my life, I have found that it is life-giving to recognize that the Creator's deepest value is to bless all the families of the world. The Creator called Jesus to gather a community that recognizes all people as equally human and the earth as our sacred trust for future generations.

We honor our own humanity when we honor the humanity of diverse people.

I wish to thank all the leaders of wisdom communities who have shaped this work: Buddhist, Christian, Muslim, Jewish, Sikh, Hindu, Atheist, Agnostic, Zoroastrian, Indigenous, and many more.

I particularly wish to thank:

- Father William Treacy and Rabbi Raphael Levine for their legacy of leadership in building unity within the human family.
- Professor Paul Ingram who embodied curiosity and integrity.
- Professor Phil Hefner who encouraged a young seminarian to keep thinking.
- Each of the congregations I have served: Grace Lutheran, Salem Lutheran, Celebration Lutheran, Christ Episcopal, St. James Episcopal, St. Paul's Episcopal, The Catacomb Churches, and St. Philip's Episcopal.
- Dan Erlander for his vision, integrity, humility, and humor.
- Elders Kay Knott and Jay Bowen of the Upper Skagit Tribe for their friendship and teachings.
- Rabbi Daniel Wiener of Temple De Hirsch Sinai in Seattle for his leadership and wise questions.
- Aneelah Afzali of the Muslim Association of Puget Sound for her leadership and partnership for our common humanity.
- Rabbi Yohanna Kinberg and Imam Adam Jamal for their insight and wisdom.
- Pastor Andy Rutrough for our many conversations.
- Viveka Hall-Holt for her assistance in the writing and editing of this work.
- Pastor April Boyden for proofreading.
- Pastor Karen Van Stee for reviewing the book in its late stages.
- The Paths to Understanding staff: Ean Olsen, Carla Pender-

ock, Viveka Hall-Holt, and Ana Mehmood.

• The Paths to Understanding Board for their support, encouragement, and feedback: Gregg Davidson, Jeff Renner, Liz Gimmestad, Rachel Taber-Hamilton, Jennifer Bereskin, Sumia Dakhil, Bridgette Scheppat, Allison Flash, and Jasmit Singh.

This work is nothing unless we move from our books and education hours into public partnerships in which we know, work with, and publicly honor people of all cultures, wisdom traditions, and economic situations. A crucial first step toward action is to become clearer about our "why." The key is to take that "why" and leap into a relationship with others who are leaping with us – even if we only see each other after our own lonely leap. The discussion questions, activities, and additional resources on our website can help us move into relationship and action.

We do not have to live divided from one another. We can go together into our communities and create a better future together.

Download Discussion Questions, Action Steps, & Resources:
https://pathstounderstanding.org/gdl/

A Brief Word about Biblical Interpretation

In the late 1970's, a quiet revolution in Biblical interpretation began. A few Biblical scholars explored using the tools of cultural anthropology to study the Christian Scriptures. In addition to other tools such as the original languages, ancient history, and the literary study of the texts, they wanted to understand the culture of the day. They recognized that when we read the Christian Scriptures, we are doing cross-cultural work.

They studied ancient texts, looking for clues about the 1st century culture of Jesus. They also went into rural villages in Israel and Palestine and asked locals to interpret many stories. They used some tools of cultural anthropology to deeply respect the texts in their original contexts. Over time, they began to gain a sense of the culture of Jesus' day and how it compared to our own.

Now, this is not about gaining certainty in interpreting a text. We can never be entirely certain about the meaning of a text written today, let alone one from two thousand years ago.

Still, we need to consider that Jesus grew up in a certain time and place. He spoke languages. He used terms of his day, referencing the technology and stories that were known to most people in his time. Yet, it seems clear to many theologians and Biblical scholars that the church lost much of the context of Jesus' day in the early centuries of the church. Without that context, we often apply own cultural contexts onto the text itself.

Bruce Malina, Richard Rohrbaugh, John Pilch, and others put together resources to help us get in the ballpark of interpretations around Jesus' time. While we can never be sure we have it totally right, there are certain traditional interpretations that we can now understand to be inaccurate. Further, the stories in the Bible were meant to have multiple interpretations. But this does not mean that they mean whatever we want.

Some Christians claim to be "conservative," while others see themselves as "liberal." Neither of these are of much interest to me. Often, arguments between these two perspectives are more about intergroup rivalry than a search for a humble and honest interpretation of the Bible. We quite naturally apply our desire to confirm our current viewpoint onto the text. The question is rather one of faithfulness to Jesus, the Jesus who lived in a 1st century, Roman-occupied, Jewish context. If the work of faithfulness challenges or changes some of my own assumptions, well then, so be it. If it challenges or changes yours, I hope you will lean into the discomfort.

I do not mean that every part of our tradition should easily be set aside. We need to hold our interpretations and traditions together. On the other hand, just because Christians have taught something for a long time doesn't mean these teachings are faithful to Jesus. Following Jesus' example, we use tradition, reason, and experience to critique how we understand and live out our tradition today. We will need to set aside some teachings and practices in order to be as faithful to the vision of Jesus as we can.

To do this, we are invited to continually become more aware of how we read and interpret scripture based on our own culture or unexamined thinking.

Here is an example that might help illustrate how we may be invited to grow in our interpretations: What does it mean when Mary sat at Jesus' feet in Luke 10? For centuries, people have interpreted this text to mean that Mary was a faithful female follower in a subservient position to the male Jesus. Martha, on the other hand, was seen as a disrespectful woman "distracted" by her insignificant woman's work.

Through the work these and other scholars have done using the social science approach, we now understand this passage differently. In that century, women were not accepted as teachers or leaders in the public square or the Temple. Sitting at Jesus' feet was a position that meant Mary was accepted into Jesus' rabbinical school. Martha sees this and she knows that severe punishment awaited people who broke these social and religious norms. Martha was a courageous friend and leader who was saying, "Are you sure you want to do this? Do you know that they will punish you both and the household besides?"

Jesus' response is not a put down of Martha but a way to say,

"Yes, we know we are breaking the rules–because I believe women should be among the leaders and teachers in society." Sadly, the larger cultural view that only men could lead and teach eventually overcame the church, and this interpretation was lost.

Many scholars are now highly confident that this interpretation of Mary as a rabbi-in-training is "in the ballpark" of faithfulness.[1] It can and should be used to support the church welcoming the leadership of people of all genders.

Once we get a better feel for the context of Jesus' words and actions, we can then see the direction that he is leading us. This gives us a clue as to how Jesus continues to lead in our context. Striving to understand Jesus' context and our own contexts is critical to discerning how to respond faithfully to his leadership.

Today, the social sciences are among the most important tools Biblical scholars use to interpret scripture. They don't always agree on everything, but they do agree on many things.

In 1999, I began to read the work of social science scholars. As I prepared to preach each week, I read their work and began to gain a feel for the cultural landscape of the 1st century, Roman occupied, and Jewish context of Jesus' ministry. It challenged and changed many of my views.

Again, I don't claim to be right. I only claim to strive to have a faithful-and-open-to-revision understanding of Jesus' ministry and how it might apply today.

I reference 1st century culture often in this book. There are so many references that I have decided not to footnote each one. It would simply be too much! However, I want to honor the work of these and other scholars and invite you to begin or continue your own journey toward understanding Jesus in his context of Judea two thousand years ago.

I encourage you to read the *Social Science Commentaries* published by Fortress Press. Start with the one on the Synoptic Gospels.[2]

I have learned much from N. T. Wright's trilogy *Christian Origins and the Question of God*, Sally McFague, Wes Howard Brook, Cynthia Moe-Lobeda, Marcus Borg, and Walter Wink. There are so many more. I have also learned from engaging with people in Bible study, wondering with them how the texts might have been understood by the first to hear them.

We cannot know with certainty. Indeed, certainty is wise to avoid because it often comes with an unwillingness to learn, risk, grow, and love.

However, I think we are likely to be nearer to understanding what Jesus' leadership meant as we become informed about the likely cultural, historical, and linguistic context in which he lived. To do so takes Jesus seriously.

Section One: The Meaning of One Creator

Key Question: What does our wisdom tradition propose about the unity of humanity?

Summary: The focus of this section is what the Abrahamic traditions teach about the unity of human beings. I'll begin by describing the challenges we face today and framing the language we use to describe interfaith work. I'll address the meaning behind monotheism, which is central to this book. Finally, I'll talk about how we are centered as Christians in our baptismal identity—and that part of being beloved of God is that we can grow and change.

Chapter One: Our God, Not Yours

My first powerful memories were of my Mother coming home from the hospital with a diagnosis of multiple sclerosis. We expected her imminent death, judging from others in our town who were diagnosed with it.

My home church was a haven for me. Pastor Walla was kind. His wife Mary gave all of us children hugs when we came to church. I felt embraced there in many ways. Sitting in the second pew on the right, I could see the stained-glass window of Jesus carrying a lamb, with the mother walking beside. This image promised that I could be carried, even if my Mother could no longer carry me.

I learned about God's creation, God's love in Jesus for all people, and the Holy Spirit's continuing presence. I learned to respect the power of tradition to both humble and empower us for a life of meaning and service.

My great grandfather, Jens Wiggen, immigrated from Norway to the United States in the 1870s. Famine and overpopulation led Jens to get in an eighteen-foot wooden boat with twelve other people and cross the Atlantic for the promise of free farmland. Getting his six hundred acres, he joined other Norwegians to start Selbu Lutheran church, named in honor of their hometown. The story of his arrival told by my family never mentioned the Palus Peoples who were forcibly removed from their homes in the fertile Palouse hills.

My church, while offering many good lessons, also limited my capacity to relate to people of diverse cultures and traditions in ways I am still grappling with:

- Christianity is the only way to God
- Christianity is God's only way to us
- Christians are superior
- Love is primarily expressed in making others to be like us

- God cannot accept non-Christians, even though God would like to
- God gave this land to us
- Counting down to Jesus' second coming and his destruction of the earth

My church taught that Jesus came to the earth because the Jewish people had been unfaithful to their covenant with God. Thus God had to find a new way to offer salvation to humans. The new covenant of the Christians superseded the old covenant with the people of Israel. The old promises were broken and required a conversion to Christianity for Jews to once again have access to God.

I also learned things in the parking lot. If Sunday School was primarily a place of women's teaching, the men's teaching took place in a circle in the parking lot after church. After singing "Jesus loves the little children, all the children of the world," I would regularly hear racial slurs toward people of Indigenous, Jewish, Black, and Asian communities. I never heard anyone push back on this. They assumed their status-keeping system was given by God.

This added an often-silent-but-always-present whisper of "white Christians are superior" to the teachings above. None of this seemed incongruent to them with our tradition's teachings of One Creator, God's call to be a blessing to all nations, the freeing of the Israelites from slavery, and a Jesus who honored the Samaritans.

God belonged to us, not to all. "Our Father" meant the God who belonged to Christians.

It took many years for me to realize that I was raised in a culture in which White Christian supremacy played a large role. This is not to say the people at my church were part of hate groups. Very few of them joined the Aryan Nation's organization that grew and quickly died in my hometown. It is also important to say that my home church, like many churches, organizations, and the culture as a whole, have changed much in these years. I am writing about my experience of them as a child. This same White Christian supremacy could be found in other churches in town, in our county, and in our country. It was just in the air.

In some ways, this supremacy was not theological, even when theology was used to justify or promote it. Christians practice theology when we critique our worldviews. Supremacy could accept no critique. We were the "good ones," and others were not. That's all we needed to know.

Even with their supremacist teachings, my church was also supportive in many ways to our family. They were kind in many ways to people who were different. A person from my church even took us to visit a Jewish Temple in Spokane so we could understand Jewish people better.

Humans are complicated and full of contradictions. I still love my home congregation.

The Doorway

I knew my Mother had a chronic, debilitating illness. I knew, in a pre-verbal way, that this status-keeping system of supremacy was applied to my Mother and thus our family. A member of the church made this clear to me when she confronted me in the doorway to the church sanctuary. She told me, "If your family were better Christians, your Mother would not be sick." I was seven years old. I felt shame. Internally, I resisted what she said. How could the Jesus who carried the lamb, who promised to carry me, create the illness in my Mother because we weren't good enough Christians?

My Father was among the youngest in his family. My grandfather John promised that Dad was going to run the farm. This promise kept my Dad from finishing high school or going to college. But Grandpa sold the farm. My Father and Mother bought a grocery store in town, the smaller of two stores. Given the march of mechanization in farming, which led to ever larger farms and fewer farmhands, Lacrosse didn't need two stores. Eventually, the store went out of business and my family went through bankruptcy. To survive, my Dad reluctantly took a custodian job at the school.

Losing the farm led to a loss of status for our family. I remember when my Father swept the floors on the basketball court at halftime. Some of the high-status farmers would mock him by yelling, "Let's go, Bruce." The others would laugh. My Dad would smile as if he was in on the joke. The status-keeping system did not only apply to the "others" outside our White community. The jovial brutality of supremacy tore us apart not only from people of other cultures and traditions but also from within.

In my bones I knew this status-keeping system was wrong. I couldn't wait to get out of Lacrosse. I knew that once I left, the story of my Mother's illness, our loss of the farm, our bankruptcy and all our negative history would be washed away. I knew that if I worked hard, I would have many opportunities, amplified by my status as a white male Christian.

Neighbors in Faith

I began my journey to become a pastor at the Lutheran School of Theology at Chicago. Hyde Park was the most diverse neighborhood in the United States at the time. Going to the store or for a walk was an intercultural experience. For a child of a town of 300 people, this was both daunting and amazing.

Our professors had ongoing conversations with Hebrew scholars. Ralph Klein taught us that the Jewish faith "continued to be new." They advocated a move away from the terms "new and old testaments." They saw that while Christians were free to interpret the Hebrew Scriptures, we also could respect and learn from Jewish interpretations.

In seminary, I learned the role that Lutheran churches and Martin Luther's writings played in Germany during the Holocaust. As we sat at lunch that day, we were unusually quiet. After a time I said, "If I ever see something like that happen when I'm a pastor, I'm not going to be silent." Many around the table took the same vow.

In 2012 I began to serve an Episcopal Church in Marysville, WA. Fred Wade served as the church treasurer. He introduced me to some local Muslims. He loved the chicken-fried steak they made at their restaurant. In 2014, I engaged in some interfaith conversations with Muslims and Buddhists in Marysville. As word of this work spread, I was invited to come to a military town with my Muslim friend to help reduce the anti-Muslim bigotry there. This community had been traumatized from the wars in Iraq and Afghanistan, and it showed. From the stage, I saw the rage and fear that some brought into that room. As we did more events around the area, I heard the same questions, worded in the same way, in almost the same order, everywhere we went. I read about a $30 million-a-year network of organizations using every means possible to make Muslims appear as less than human in the eyes of America-loving and Jesus-loving people. This reminded me of the dehumanization of Jewish communities that paved the way for the Holocaust—and many other genocides.

We held events in four other towns, and I saw the same fear and hate at each event. Within the year, I organized 11 other events around Western Washington. I saw a candidate for the US presidency reference a "report" from a recognized hate group saying that over 80 percent of Muslims approved of political violence. The candidate wanted to ban Muslims from entering the country. Verified research showed that the hate group's "report" was not true, but fear is powerful. Fear that what we love is going to be harmed can be turned into the desire to do harm. This kind of fear becomes perceived permission and even a moral obligation to engage in violence toward a group.

As a Lutheran Pastor, I am part of a tradition that has done such harm. Traditions inspire with values and stories. Being part of one obligates us to look at how those in our tradition's past have fallen short and behave differently ourselves. At these events, I was seeing something like the dehumanization of the Jewish people in Europe happening to Muslims in the US. Dehumanization of one group, if unchecked, leads to the dehumanization of other groups.

As a pastor, I spent many hours reading and studying scriptures—often in conversation with other pastors. I began to feel the contradictions between my early Sunday School teachings and what I was reading in the Christian Scriptures. I felt the tensions between the stated values of our tradition and the enslavement of 11 million people from Africa and the theft of Indigenous lands—including those on which my home church was built. I began to relate more honestly to people of different cultures and experiences. I began to read cross-cultural interpretations of the Christian Scriptures and slowly, painfully, began to sense something different from my earlier understanding of Jesus.

Ervin Staub, a Jewish survivor of the Holocaust, writes that the difference between nations that engage in genocide and those that don't are people in the majority who stand up and say, "No!"

While talking to a Muslim friend, I said that someone needs to go into Christian churches to prepare them to stand up in public with their Muslim neighbors. As I said this, I felt great pressure on my body and I heard my own voice say, "I think I need to do this." After conversations with my family and friends, other pastors, and bishops in both Lutheran and Episcopal churches, I started Neighbors in Faith. We engaged with Christian Congregations, introduced them to Muslims, held public events, did a multi-city road show, and created animated videos. As a white, Christian, male pastor, I knew it was my responsibility to do what I could to encourage people to stand up with our Muslim neighbors-in-faith.

Each time after I worked with Muslims in these public settings, I would ask them a painful question for reflection: "How did I disadvantage you today?" At first, they didn't want to answer, so as not to hurt my feelings. As trust increased, they learned that I could hear it. They realized I was willing to work on my own supremacist attitudes. I spent many sleepless nights after those events as I reflected on how I was being invited to change. Now I realize that this pain is a not an extra burden placed upon me–this pain is inherent in my baptism at Selbu Lutheran Church on November 15, 1964. The Apostle Paul knew such pain as well and called daily baptism "death and rebirth."

I began to recognize that, when I dehumanize other peoples and cultures, I am participating in my own harm. When I stand by passively, I am being passive to my own humanity. Connecting to the humanity of others connects me to my own as a child of One Creator.

Ironically, I learned this in Sunday School, too. Even the men in the circle in the parking lot seemed at times to suggest something like this. It was like they could not see the contradictions. But then, dear reader, we human beings often struggle to do so.

Many Faiths

In 2020, we merged Neighbors in Faith with the Treacy Levine Center to become Paths to Understanding. The Treacy Levine Center was begun out of Rabbi Raphael Levine's and Father William Treacy's partnership on the ground-breaking TV show *Challenge*. In that show, a Catholic Priest, Jewish Rabbi, and Protestant Pastor talked as equals about the challenging topics of the day. Their show was revolutionary, controversial, and inspiring.

In this new partnership, as well as in the work of Neighbors in Faith, I came in contact with people of many wisdom traditions and cultures. I had lively conversations with Jews, Muslims, Buddhists, Atheists, Agnostics, Zoroastrians, Hindus, Sikhs, Indigenous people, and many other traditions. The cycle of baptismal death and rebirth continued in me. Witnessing other traditions helped me see my tradition more clearly. Conversations with these insightful, powerful, and compassionate people, as a part of my commitment to Jesus, have led me to write this book.

Three Questions

During the COVID 19 pandemic, I held conversations with hundreds of people of diverse traditions. I asked three questions:

- What do you see happening in the United States right now?
- What does your tradition offer as an analysis of our situation?
- What does your tradition offer as a strategy to bring us to a better situation?

Everyone said something about how we are living in an age of dehumanization, being torn asunder, and that the outcome of this was increased violence. They said that this could lead to a complete societal breakdown. Leaders brought many different analyses from their traditions. Yet, there were many similarities, including in-group/out-group tensions along with our capacity to justify ourselves and our positions by denying new information. Most of us shared similar strategies of gathering people of diverse traditions and cultures to:

- know each other
- do good with and for each other
- honor each other in public

Paths to Understanding's initiative, "Let's Go Together," grew out of this collective wisdom.

As we developed Let's Go Together, I realized that most Christians had, like me, grown up with a kind of supremacy in the society that was often ignored by and sometimes authorized by the church. To invite us to participate in work with people of diverse cultures and traditions, some baptismal work is necessary. This work is a response to faith in Jesus. This baptismal work reconnects us to our own humanity and the humanity of each other.

As I have walked this path with people of many traditions, I have rediscovered how the Christian tradition encourages us to work with and honor people of all traditions through:

- the meaning of One Creator
- the call of Abraham
- Jesus as a monotheist
- the core values of the Abrahamic tradition
- Jesus' vision of the Kindom of God
- God's healing of the universe leading to action and hope

We will explore these in this book.

While, in some ways my church failed to carry me, Jesus has picked me up. He is carrying me, like a weary and growing lamb, to running waters with lambs of other flocks.

Chapter Two: The Challenges We Face

If you are like me, you're feeling anxious about the divisions in our society. We see these divisions in our families, friends, and coworkers. We often have trouble speaking respectfully with people from different groups. We are experiencing a lack of trust in each other and are tempted to withdraw from each other.

Our polarization is so powerful that recent surveys have revealed that 4 percent of the US population is willing to participate in a violent demonstration. Alarmingly high percentages of all political parties believe that political violence "may be necessary to save our country."[3]

Many things have contributed to this:

- chronic loneliness
- wealth and income inequity
- climate change driven scarcity
- racist policies, ideas, and attitudes
- historical trauma
- technology driven change—especially in communications
- nationalist movements that claim people with diverse traditions cannot live together productively and in peace

Taken together, these trends threaten the functioning and future of our beautiful democracy and the relative peace of our beloved communities.

Two Challenges

We face two major challenges:

Our nation is dangerously polarized. Social cohesion, the glue of trust that holds us together, is decreasing. This polarization is already leading to an increase in political violence. Political violence is always wrong, no matter its ideological excuses. Communities of wisdom can play a role in rebuilding our social cohesion by building relationships with other communities—especially those with whom we disagree.

Our nation is dangerously unequal. Some groups of people do not have the same chance to realize the promise of "Life, Liberty and the pursuit of Happiness." This lack of equity is a form of violence. It creates a social hierarchy that diminishes the vision of "we the people, in order to form a more perfect union." Communities of wisdom, especially Christians who are in the majority, can play a role in working for equity for all people.

We don't have to live this way. We don't have to live polarized and unequal. What can we do to make a difference?

To find an effective strategy, we need wisdom about what makes human beings tick. Wisdom traditions across the world, what we often refer to as "religions," offer insight into both how human beings are vulnerable to destructive behaviors and how to activate our positive potential.

I see two primary dynamics at work in both polarization and inequity:

- Exclusive In-Grouping: The assumption that one's group is the best
- Dehumanization: A process in which other in-groups are seen as less than human, thus appropriate targets of violence

Rural areas are an important part of this conversation. Studies show that counties with the greatest demographic and cultural changes recently were more likely to send someone to the January 6th insurrection because "people of color are gaining rights faster than white people."[4] While this certainly is not a logical framing of the problem, as rights are not a limited good, it is how some people are reacting. These reactions may be amplified as rural areas, smaller towns, and cities grow in both population and in cultural diversity. For instance, it is estimated that Western Washington's population will increase by two million people by 2050. We need to prepare these communities to know, respect, and work with new neighbors.

We have seen examples of these challenges in Western Washington and beyond:

- reaction to mosque building projects in Mukilteo and Snohomish
- physical attacks on people of religious, cultural, and racial minorities
- vandalism and arson at places of worship, including Jewish, Sikh, African American Christian, Roman Catholic, Muslim, Jehovah's Witness, Latter Day Saints, and more
- continued violence against American Asians, Indigenous, and LGBTQIA+ communities

Our differences are being exaggerated. We are not seeing each other as we are because we are overwhelmed by negative news about each other. Most Americans hold many values[5] in common:

- individual freedoms such as freedom of speech
- every citizen should be able to vote
- respecting American political institutions and laws

I saw these challenges and in conversation with many leaders I began to see a strategy for how we can respond.

A Strategic Response

What do we do when human beings are estranged from one another, when our trust in each other is low, and when we see each other as enemies? Wisdom traditions offer insight and wisdom to find a way forward. After much consultation with leaders of diverse traditions, I have come to believe that the power of *in-person and locally focused experiences* are more powerful than media and social media. Trust will grow as diverse groups get together and

- Eat and share stories
- Work for the common good
- Show up in public together[6]

When we do these things together, powerful things happen. We begin to build our trust in each other.

Some might say that to engage in these partnerships we need to set aside our own traditions. I don't agree with that! I believe in both working together out of shared values and increasing in commitment to our own tradition.

When communities of wisdom, like churches, temples, mosques, and other cultural groups build a future together, it is a powerful witness: Our diverse cultures and traditions are an asset to a positive, beautiful future.

Hope

I understand that many people are experiencing a loss of hope and a sense of despair about our future. I feel that, too!

A friend of mine was feeling despair and hopelessness. It weighed on her in nearly every moment. Then she read an article about how she could use her nursing skills to benefit Ukrainian refugees in Poland. She signed up, went to Poland, and found something she thought she would never feel again: **hope, meaning, and joy.**

It was wonderful to see her despair lifted. She said that after a rest, she would find some other way to share her gifts. She recognized that while the impact of her actions was small, together we can make a substantial difference in our future.

If we wait for the feeling of hope before we begin to act together, hope may not come. Wisdom traditions across the world remind us that sometimes action leads to feelings. **Experience can lead to hope**.

We don't need to go to Poland to do this. We can act together in our own neighborhoods and communities. Our wisdom communities and cultural groups can act together and counter the narrative of the nationalist movements. We can live peacefully with each other.

I believe the Creator is calling us to create that positive future for ourselves, our children, and our planet.

Will Christians step up to do our part to meet these challenges? To do so, we need to recognize that it is faithful to Jesus to work with people of diverse wisdom traditions. That is the subject of this book.

Chapter Three: Religion, Interfaith, and Wisdom Traditions

I was on the street one day. I was wearing my clergy collar, and a man said to me: "Your God is the source of most wars." He was angry but was also respectful of me as a person. I understood that his anger came from his love and his values. I said to him, "I think another 'G' word is the source of most wars." He asked me, "What is that?" I said, "Greed." I went on to say, "But certainly religious folk have often blessed this greed along with the violence it creates and has benefited from it. We are responsible for the times when we did that." He conceded the point. He also thanked me for taking responsibility for the failed promise of religious traditions. We parted well.

Increasing numbers of people in the United States are distancing themselves from religion. They associate it with war, division, arrogance, and the blessing of unjust systems. A very common orthodoxy is that religion is the primary source of most wars.

There is an anti-religious bigotry among some in the United States. This bigotry implies that if we just got rid of religion, the world would be better. From Bill Maher, Sam Harris, and Ron Reagan, Jr., we see a concentrated dehumanization of people of wisdom traditions. In doing so, they engage in the same behavior they profess to hate in wisdom traditions.

While religious traditions do sometimes play a role in wars, several historical reviews have found that religion plays a role, but not always the primary role, in between only 6 percent and 15 percent of all wars. [7]

Certainly, religious traditions can play a role in-group/out-group distrust and even violence. People of religious faith need to take responsibility for the times we have:

- blessed unjust systems and violence against others

- passively stood by while others suffered
- benefitted from the oppression of others
- denied our responsibility for making the world a better place
- claimed to be better than others

However, this is also true for non-religious groups. The 20th century was the least religious century in the history of the world. Yet, in that century, over two-hundred-and-sixty million[8] people were killed in genocides–often by those who opposed religious traditions.

Historian William Cavanaugh, in his book *The Myth of Religious Violence*, traces how many European rulers sought to blame religion for the wars over land they started. This was really a piece of propaganda that benefited the emerging nation-states by saying they were the solution to the problem of religion. This propaganda continues to work in our day.

In his book *Big Gods*, Ara Norenzayan used social science research on how belief in a moral universe through religion impacts our behavior toward others. He found that people of religious faith across the world were more likely to be kind to out-group people because of their faith. To be fair, he also found that secular societies with democratic governments also fared well in these tests!

The reality is that all human beings can participate in the good and the bad. Traditions are important, as they give us a grounding in how to be human beings in the world. But people of every tradition have a "batting average." We often claim that our group is unreservedly good with a few exceptions, and other groups are mostly bad with a few exceptions. Most traditions remind us that these claims are dangerous.

As Jesus said:

> How can you say to your neighbor, "Friend, let me take out the speck in your eye," when you yourself do not see the log in your own eye? You hypocrite, first take the log out of your own eye, and then you will see clearly to take the speck out of your neighbor's eye.
> Luke 6:42

As the Apostle Paul wrote:

> All have sinned and fall short of the glory of God.

Romans 3:23

Paul included himself and his community in this analysis. All people have fallen short of the love of God, neighbor, self, and care for the creation. Self-critique is an important part of the Christian tradition. The work of prophets, or truth-tellers, is important. Through them, God invites us to love and be ourselves more fully.

A More Equal Space

The word "religion" is notoriously difficult to define because people use it in lots of different ways. Some use it referring to belief in a supernatural power or powers. Others use it to refer to a particular tradition organized into a system of beliefs. Yet, to others, it refers to groups of people who gather over time in communities and institutions. Many others refer to it as a way of life or a set of practices. This difficulty in defining religion is part of why we at Paths to Understanding don't use it very often.

The word religion comes from the Latin word "religio," from which our term ligament comes. The religio of a community is the story that forms the connective tissue of the society. This religio tells people who we are, what is important for us to do, and who is included as important.

It seems to me that the religion in the United States today is that human beings are *homo economicus*: Humans are gladiators fighting to see who can produce and consume the most within a free-market economy that can grow infinitely.[9] We say that the one who dies with the most toys wins. Time is money, the church should run like a business, etc.

When we look back at previous eras, we often are amazed. "How could people believe that a King was put in place by God? How could people believe that the Divine approved of enslaving people?"

The problem is that when we are in a religion, living in a story about who we are, we often have a hard time questioning its assumptions. We tend to see our story as "just the way things are." This is true of all people, whether we are part of a historical wisdom tradition or not. The practice of theology is taking a look at these assumptions and how they shape human beings and societies.

A Jewish rabbi, Muslim sheik, and Christian pastor, who call themselves the Three Interfaith Amigos, shared some wisdom about how self-critique is an important part of our traditions in our TV show, Challenge 2.0.

> Ted Falcon: Sometimes I think there's a difference between truth with a small "t" and Truth with a capital "T." Truth with a small "t" has to do with an event or an incident, something that is time specific, place specific. We could argue, did it happen? Did it not happen? We could look at it from this perspective, that perspective, it could be competing narratives. To try to get everybody to agree on a small truth is not going to happen. And so there has to be a larger vessel to hold various small truth "t's. And on a scientific level, there is no fact because it's all hypothesis, people don't understand this. It's always unfolding. Big "T" represents the universals. Like we really don't argue about awakening to love. We don't argue about awakening to more compassion and compassionate action. We don't really argue about experiencing ourselves as one common family on one shared planet. And it makes a big difference when we start focusing on truth with a capital "T."

> Jamal Rahman: This reminds me of a wonderful insight, a spiritual insight about gratitude. It is said that if somebody, for example, Jamal, gives you a beautiful, expensive hat to wear, thank the small "g," the giver. But don't forget to thank the big "G," the one who gave you the head to put the hat on.

> Dave Brown: I think when we talk about the big "T," that would be another area for real dialogue between people and how they understand what the ultimate Truth is. What is the Truth that undergirds their reality?

Martin Luther, a theologian who founded the Lutheran Christian tradition, said, "Your God is whatever you fear, love, and trust." In other words, look at what matters to you most, and you will see what your ultimate concern, your "god," is. **Look at what freaks you out if it were to change–that is your god.** The role of prophets in the Hebrew tradition was to help their community confront the differences between their stated values and the reality of their communal life. This is a strength. Human beings and human communities express both strength and commitment to our values when we can face how we fall short of living them out. My seminary professors showed this strength by teaching about how Lutherans contributed to the Holocaust. Their critique of our own tradition was itself faithful to our tradition.

Redefining Interfaith

Many times, work across lines of tradition is referred to as "interfaith" or "multi-faith." Interfaith implies conversation between traditions. Multi-faith seems to imply more of a partnership between traditions out of shared values. The problem here is that the word "faith" is not a universal concept. To use that term then imposes some Christian assumptions on people who either don't use the term or who use it differently.

The choice to use the term "wisdom tradition" can be a more useful and neutral term to describe what we mean. We do, however, live in the real world where the terms "multi-faith" and "interfaith" are used. I still use them in public so that people can understand the kind of work we do. Here some definitions I like to use:

Wisdom Tradition: A set of remembered stories, practices, deep truths, probing questions, and a capacity for self-critique exploring how human beings can live with meaning in community and care for the earth. These include Buddhist, Hindu, Jewish, Sikh, Christian, Muslim, Taoist, Indigenous, Agnostic, Atheist, Humanist, and many other traditions.

Communities of Wisdom: Local or regional groups gathered around a particular wisdom tradition.

I believe that wisdom traditions offer gifts for the common good. By partnering with each other based on our shared values, we can contribute to a more peaceful, hopeful, and positive future.

When we partner through our shared values, we proclaim our values are more important than inter-group rivalry–that our common humanity is more important than our differences. While we are part of one particular in-group, we are also a part of one larger human family.

In the Christian tradition, the idea of One Creator is central to recognizing that we are part of this human family that we are to work with other traditions and honor one another in public.

Chapter Four: Human Unity
and Divine Oneness

As humans developed, we survived and thrived within groups. This is so much the case that we humans are often willing to risk ourselves individually for the good of the group. Groups developed ways to find food, build shelter, tend the ill, pass on teachings, and make clothing. They also found ways to tell right away who was and who was not a part of their in-group.

One way that we can see the lasting strength of in-groups today is in sports. I grew up in Washington State, so I am a part of the Seattle Seahawks in-group. I love them, and I dislike other teams. One day, I was visiting Pittsburgh. As soon as the cab driver heard I was from Seattle, we felt an instant but friendly rivalry. But, if I had been raised in Pittsburgh, I most likely would have loved the Steelers. It is amazing how strong these feelings of intergroup rivalry are, even over something as silly as professional sports teams.

Groups naturally develop traditions, stories, practices, deep truths, and probing questions about what it means to be human. These stories often include some kind of god, spirit, or divine force who created them, guides them, and encompasses them.

But what happens when our group meets another group with a different language, wisdom tradition, or conception of the divine? One possibility is to see the other in-group as less than human because they don't share our language, tradition, or ideas.

Recognizing Others as Human

Throughout history, many groups engaged each other in peaceful and cooperative ways. But when they got into conflict, sometimes they saw their gods as competing up in the heavens while they competed on the ground. In some cultures, the assumption was that each in-group has its own god. This meant that when the in-groups fought, the gods fought. If the gods fought, then rivalry and violence were inherent in the universe and could not be avoided. It was us versus them, dark versus light, a zero-sum game with winners and losers fighting over scarce resources. But then inspiration came: What if there is one Creator who made all in-groups? Then we are not children of competing gods but children of one Creator. We are related. This encourages cooperation and a sense of unity even as it is expressed in diversity. This encourages groups to see our conflicts as temporary problems that can be overcome.

Monotheism is the idea that there is one Creator. Monotheism was one attempt to deal with exclusive in-grouping, dehumanization, and the violence that results from them. By making the claim that there is one Creator, wisdom traditions encourage people in one in-group to recognize people in other in-groups as human.

> So God created humankind in his image,
> in the image of God, he created them;
> male and female, he created them.
> Genesis 1:27

The idea that a Creator made two human beings from whom all humans are descended means that we all share great, great, great (. . .) grandparents–we are all a part of one human family. Each person is made in the image of God, and we honor the Creator by honoring and loving them. We are part of smaller in-groups, but all human beings are a part of the larger human family.

Rabbi Levine and Father Treacy, our organization's founders, worked to bring unity in the human family.

Monotheism's primary lesson is to recognize people in other in-groups as human beings created by the same God. Respecting our Creator, then, means respecting all that God has made:

- humans
- animals
- plants
- our shared ecosystems

Just as God intentionally made many kinds of plants and animals, God made a diversity of human cultures and traditions. This is not a problem but rather a necessary and good feature of the creation. The same is true of our bodies. We each have one unified body, and it is the diversity of our cells that makes our lives possible. Diversity does not negate unity; it makes unity possible. Life itself requires and consists of cooperative diversity.

As the Holy Quran puts it:

> O humankind, We have created you from a male and
> a female and have made you into nations and tribes
> for you to know one another.
> Holy Quran 49:13[10]

Imam Adam Jamal gives his interpretation of this verse in a conversation about how wisdom traditions work together:

> Imam Adam Jamal: I wanted to just kind of stick to some of the basics. And what you'll notice is that Islam teaches a lot of the same things that Christianity and Judaism teach about all of humanity and all of mankind.

> So, the first verse I wanted to share was a verse from the Quran, chapter 49, verse number 13. . . (the Quran is this book that was revealed to the Prophet Muhammad, peace be upon him, by angel Gabriel. That's what we, as Muslims, that's what we believe.) And, so, one verse from that book is, "O mankind, we created you from a single male and a single female and made you into nations and tribes that you may know each other. And the most honorable of you in the sight of God is the one that is the most righteous." And so, in this verse, what I took away from this verse when it comes to our topic today, is this idea of us being one humanity and we are all going back to our original, I guess, beginnings. Adam and Eve, the story of Adam and Eve, going back to that and going back to this idea that we're all from the same, stemming from that same seed, and so for all of us to be this one humanity is very important.

> In the Quran, God talks to people that are in, I guess, as you said, Terry, the in-group, those believers in the in-group. And then he also addresses all of mankind, like he does in this verse, which is "all mankind, we created you as male and female," and so that address in the Quran kind of leads Muslims to think about, well, okay, in some places, God has talked to Muslims in

particular. So that's one side, and then the other side is an address to all of mankind, and so that kind of changes our focus for, okay, well, God isn't just talking to us, but God is talking to everyone, and he's showing us that there's a message here beyond just the message to us.

This idea of one human family created by one Creator and other ideas about the unity in diversity in human beings helped groups live near each other in peace. There is good evidence that most human communities, most of the time, were able to cooperate and live in peace with neighboring groups.[11]

Honoring Mystery

Each monotheistic tradition teaches a certain modesty about what we can claim to know about the Creator. In the Hebrew Tradition, the Creator asks Moses to go to Egypt and free those enslaved there. Moses asks, "Who should I say is sending me?"

> But Moses said to God, "If I come to the Israelites
> and say to them, 'The God of your ancestors has sent
> me to you,' and they ask me, 'What is his name?'
> what shall I say to them?" God said to Moses, "I AM
> WHO I AM."
> Exodus 3:13-14

The "I AM" is a name that speaks to the inherent mystery of life and the mystery of the Creator. Many Hebrew scholars say that it can mean "The One who is becoming" or "The One who exists." The God of his ancestors is asking Moses to act in the tradition of Abraham. The Creator is not something that we can control, define, or understand fully.

But, of course, human beings often want to do exactly that. That is why the commandment against idolatry was given. Any object, idea, or story that claims to define the "I AM" is an idol. Usually, people use idols to gain power over other people, to exclude questions, stop wondering, inhibit playfulness, or avoid necessary change. We can use idols to claim that our group has exclusive humanity. I fear that many people who believe in one God have engaged in idolatry, turning monotheism into the NFL: the National Faith League. This week, it's Moses vs. Mohammed, and next week, Jesus will take on the winner.

Many have reduced monotheism into mono-religionism.

Monotheism invites us to recognize and honor members of other in-groups as humans. Mono-religionism reduces monotheism by claiming people are only fully human if they think of the Creator as we do.

> Paul Tillich, a well-known theologian, taught this:
> We worship the God beyond our idea of God.
> Paul Tillich

The idea that we have the Creator "all figured out" is one expression of exclusive in-grouping. This puts us right back into a world of rivalry and competition, us versus them, smarty pants versus smarty pants.

What we say about or how we imagine God matters. Our words, images, and poetry help us to live our lives and live with others. Because we are made in the image of God, how we see God impacts how we understand ourselves and each other.

Just as the Hebrew Scriptures contain writings from many traditions and viewpoints, so the Christian Scriptures have four gospels and many writings that share similar and yet different views of Jesus and his significance.

As I worked to counter anti-Muslim bigotry, I taught at many congregations. I became concerned that Christians were confused about monotheism. They often responded to Tillich's quote by shaking their heads and disagreeing with him. It didn't matter how liberal or conservative a church claimed to be. Christians often tended toward mono-religionism than monotheism, that they had God figured out and that God belonged to them, not all. I sensed a desire for superiority over people of other faiths in these good-natured, church-going people. I began to realize I did, too.

Jesus was a monotheist. Jesus' leadership in the world was that of a monotheist in the tradition of Abraham, Moses, and the prophets. He respected the mystery of the I AM. He worked for unity in the human family because he believed that one Creator made humans and we all share two ancient ancestors.

Not Just Monotheism

Monotheism is an understanding of God inspired to help humans recognize themselves as a part of a diverse yet unified humanity and creation because of a unity in the Divine.

It is important to say that polytheistic traditions, that is, traditions that believe in multiple gods, also work to recognize the unity in diversity of humans and the creation, sometimes also talking about unity in the Divine. They do so in response to other cultural contexts and forms of exclusive in-grouping, bringing different wisdom to bear in their context and in our larger human struggle to recognize each other as human. Even though we may see the Divine differently, we can agree on our unity as human beings.

As I said, monotheism's weakness is that it can become idolatrous: imagining that there is only one true religion and using it to support unjust systems. Swami Sridharananda describes how he understands the Vedanta Hindu tradition to be speaking to our common identity as human beings.

> "Dear friends, I need your kind permission to address ourselves as the children of the divine. This is our true heritage; this is where we belong. Somewhere or other down the line we have forgotten it. And as members of the Vedanta Society, the purpose of Vedantic education is to rehabilitate ourselves to our lost glory. That is what we are here for. We are trying to expose ourselves to such man-making, character-making, noble ideas, absolving and assimilating which the quality of our personality will improve. We will no more be victims of our passions, which makes us a lesser specimen of human being, but holding onto that which will be able to grow to such a dimension, spiritually, not physically, will be able to grow to such a dimension, where we will experience the oneness with the divine. This is our true, original heritage, and that is what the Vedanta movement is all about. So let me start from this premise."
> Swami Sridharananda[12]

This Swami teaches that we are children of the divine. His insistence on the centrality of Vedanta's teaching that we are children of the divine demonstrates that traditions that are not classically understood as monotheistic can also have strong understandings of human unity and shared relationship with the divine.

As Christian monotheists, our worldview teaches us about the unity of the Creator and, thus, the unity of the creation. This belief leads us to be committed to the unity and diversity of human be-ings–no matter how others see the world, what culture they are part of, the color of their skin, who they love, or to which religion (or no religion) they belong.

One of the ways we fall short of living our values is by apply-ing our values only "if" people believe like us, only "if" they are a part of our in-group. I have learned so much through engaging with people of diverse cultures and traditions. It was through my conversations with Indigenous elders, Muslims, Jews, Sikhs, and many others that I came to see this understanding of monotheism as one strategy to recognize the unity of human beings. Engaging with them has drawn me more deeply into my own tradition. Our tradition teaches that the diversity of people and their traditions is a beautiful part of life that we can embrace because we believe in one Creator. We can join in common purpose with others who are likewise committed to the unity and diversity of all life. By do-ing this, we can be faithful to our own tradition without using the dangerous word "if."

To honor God is to honor all that God has made. One Creator means that we must work together to meet the challenges of our day. This work does not lead us away from our commitment to our own tradition, it allows us to more deeply live out our Baptismal Identity.

Chapter Five: Baptism and Identity of Belovedness

I was invited to lead the baptism of my great nephew, Jordi. He was two-and-a-half years old at the time. I led the baptism in the congregation in which I grew up. Selbu Lutheran is in the rolling hills of the Palouse country. Wheat farms surround the church, located seven miles outside the town of Lacrosse, WA. Lacrosse is home to 300 people or so. This is where I was baptized. This is where I learned of the Creator's love for me.

I began by asking the congregation a question: "Do I have the power to make God love Jordi if God doesn't want to?"

They all answered, "No."

"Pastor John," I asked, "Do you have the power to make God love Jordi if God doesn't want to?"

He laughed and said, "No!"

I asked the congregation again, "Do you all have the power to make God love Jordi if God doesn't want to?"

They all smiled, shook their heads, and said, "No."

I told them this story: Martin Luther received many letters from people asking for his advice. One day, he got a letter from a young woman whose child died in childbirth. The child died before the child could be baptized. It was normal in those days to believe that unbaptized humans cannot go to heaven when they die. In her distress and grief, she asked Luther if her child was doomed to eternal torment. He responded: "The waters of birth are baptism enough."

I went on to say that baptism does not make God love Jordi. The God we see revealed in our tradition already does. God is committed to love Jordi and does so because God chooses to. Baptism is our way to honor God's love for Jordi and for all the human family. This means that, in our baptism, we are reminded that God invites us to:

- See that our lives are accepted by God simply because God chooses to do so
- View every other human as accepted by God
- Love our neighbor as we love ourselves, holding our needs and the needs of others in tension with each other

Then, we began the baptismal liturgy. It was an honor and blessing to be there.

Jesus' Baptism

Jesus also was baptized a long time ago in the river Jordan. One after another, people went into the river, the birthplace of his people in the land, submerged in the water, and came to a new beginning.

Jesus, a step at a time, got closer to the river. I imagine that his feet hurt. Finally, it was his turn. Then, there were many more to be baptized after him.

John invited his people to repent, to find a new beginning, to change directions, to be cleansed of ways of life that were distorting their humanity, harming each other, and destroying the earth. The people knew that the way they were living under Roman occupation was destroying their lives. As the Apostle Paul later wrote,

Do not be conformed to this world, but be
transformed by the renewing of your minds so that
you may discern what is the will of God—what is
good and acceptable and perfect.
Romans 12:2

Jesus' people were being conformed by the influence of the social forces around them. The word "world" here means culture and social forces of the Roman Empire. Most likely, we would have been influenced by them as well.

John the Baptist was part of a movement to restore the people to what God intended for them and to honor their humanity. Jesus wanted in.

The Christian Scriptures tell us that at least Jesus heard these words: "This is my Son, the Beloved, with whom I am well pleased." These words have deeply formed our understanding of baptism into Christ. The call to change direction, to repent, is first grounded in something far deeper: God's affirmation of our existence and belovedness. Not only did God

- create us as a good part of a "good, and very good" creation, but in baptism, God continues to affirm our lives.
- affirm our lives, but in baptism is working to bring healing and new creation to the earth and all its life, including us.
- promise a healed, whole, and vibrant earth, but in baptism, God invites us to take part in its healing.

Jesus received this affirmation, too. God's affirmation enables and sustains our repentance, our changing direction from ways of living that destroy life.

God's affirmation of Jesus in his baptism doesn't threaten God's affirmation of us. The Creator has enough, and more than enough, affirmation and love for all of life, for all the human family, for you, and for me. There is no need to compete with others over something that is infinite, over something that God gives freely.

God's affirmation of our whole selves is what Christians call our "baptismal identity." This term does not mean that God only affirms people who are baptized (God affirms all God's children) but rather that this is the identity that we remember in the sacred ritual of baptism.

Let's take a moment here to reflect on what our baptismal identity means. Because we are affirmed in our existence, because God loves us, our identity and worth are secure. We may struggle to fully trust this, but we are secure, nonetheless. This means that we are free to learn, grow, and change. We are free to make mistakes and learn from them. We are free to grow and to encounter the growth pains that come. We are free to begin to see ourselves and others in a new way.

Our Baptism

In baptism, we remember that God affirms the very root of our life and invites us to daily death and resurrection, dying in ways that destroy or deform our lives, our neighbor's lives, and the life of the planet. In this death and resurrection, we continually move through a cycle of

- orientation
- disorientation
- new orientation

Walter Brueggemann, a Protestant Biblical scholar and theologian, proposed this cycle in his book, *Praying the Psalms.*

Baptism is paired with this cycle because:

- God affirms our lives when things seem to make sense
- God affirms our lives when things don't make sense, and we are coming apart
- God affirms our lives when we come to a new view, a new awareness, a new way

One of the strengths of wisdom traditions is how they invite people to grow in meaningful ways, like in our tradition of baptism. Imam Jamal Rahman shared this wisdom in a conversation about how his tradition encourages him toward life-long change:

> Imam Jamal Rahman: You might know that the sage poet Rumi in the 13th century, for the last 25 years, has been the most popular poet in the West. People dismiss him, saying, "He's a Sufi." Well, what is Sufi? A Sufi is just someone who practices the spirituality of Islam. Rumi is actually an Islamic theologian, and why is he so popular? Because he, like many other Sufi sages, they focus so much on the critical need, no matter what your religion, the main purpose is to really evolve into the fullness of your being by transforming your ego, opening up your heart, and being of service to God's creation. So Rumi has brought incredible popularity of this term, let's open up our hearts. . .. Rumi never wrote, rather, he just uttered by going into a trance. He says, "Please, close down speech's door, and open the window of your heart. The moon will kiss you, only through the window." And he's following a Quranic injunction. The heart is mentioned 132 times in the Quran. "Open for me, my heart." So a lot of our work today is really to find ways, it doesn't matter what your tradition, or no tradition, how can I create that inner spaciousness?

We all know that the Christian community has fallen far short of loving God, our neighbor, and God's creation. We have, like people in every generation, participated in a way of life that destroys life. We also know that this moment demands that we join Jesus in a line down by the Jordan River. It is time to open the windows of our hearts and wait for the moon to kiss us. We want a new way to live and participate in the healing and creation of the world. But even so, we rest in a secure trust that God accepts and embraces us as we continue to follow the path of Jesus.

Our Baptismal Identity

In this book, you may encounter ideas, cultures, practices, and people that challenge you. Ask yourself how you felt seeing an imam quoted here. You may see reactions in yourself that are disturbing or challenging. You may feel good about something one day and have a different reaction another day.

This all takes work.

Remembering that our lives are affirmed by God through orientation, disorientation, and a new orientation takes prayer and practice. We must nurture our trust in the Creator's affirmation. A daily spiritual practice is one way to nurture our trust.

If you already have a daily spiritual practice, keep that up.

If you don't, I am offering spiritual practices as a part of the resources on our website to help you remember your identity as one of God's holy and beloved children, a part of a good and very good creation.

Here is the basic pattern:

Remember your baptismal identity, your authentic self, make the sign of the cross, and say, "God accepts all of me."

- Take some long, slow breaths.
- Ask yourself:
  - When did I feel fully alive today?
  - When did I feel life draining away?
- Notice over time what gives you life and do more of that.
- Pray the Lord's Prayer.
- Remember your baptismal identity, make the sign of the cross, and say, "God is creating me."

While this is the basic pattern, there are many ways to remember your baptismal identity:

- Centering Prayer
- Mindful Exercise
- Journaling
- Art
- Prayer Beads

Find some brief practice that can help you remember who you are amid change and a changing world.

Wisdom traditions help us to know who we are and have a set of stories, practices, and values that guide us to a meaningful and authentic life. Whatever your tradition is, lean into it as you read through this book, and begin to engage with people of other traditions as a part of the human family.

Section One Bible Studies

Each section concludes with two short reflections on an important text in the Christian Scriptures. The first is a text that supports work with people of other traditions and cultures. The second is a text often used to say that Christians should not.

Jesus Honoring Our Common Humanity

Luke 10:25-37

Just then, a lawyer stood up to test Jesus. 'Teacher,' he said, 'what must I do to inherit eternal life?' He said to him, 'What is written in the law? What do you read there?' He answered, 'You shall love the Lord your God with all your heart, and with all your soul, and with all your strength, and with all your mind; and your neighbor as yourself.' And he said to him, 'You have given the right answer; do this, and you will live.'

But wanting to justify himself, he asked Jesus, 'And who is my neighbor?' Jesus replied, 'A man was going down from Jerusalem to Jericho and fell into the hands of robbers, who stripped him, beat him, and went away, leaving him half dead. Now, by chance, a priest was going down that road, and when he saw him, he passed by on the other side. So likewise, a Levite, when he came to the place and saw him, passed by on the other side. But a Samaritan, while travelling, came near him; and when he saw him, he was moved with pity. He went to him and bandaged his wounds, having poured oil and wine on them. Then he put him on his own animal, brought him to an inn, and took care of him. The next day, he took out two denarii, gave them to the innkeeper, and said, "Take care of him, and when I come back, I will repay you whatever more you spend." Which of these three, do you think, was a neighbor to the man who fell into the hands of the robbers?'

He said, 'The one who showed him mercy.' Jesus said to him, 'Go and do likewise."

Reflection

Samaritans and Jews were often at odds with each other in the 1st century. While they shared the first five books of the Hebrew scripture, they had different traditions and cultures. They often dehumanized each other. For example, Jewish folk believed that Samaritan territory was unclean. Thus, they avoided it or brushed off the dirt when they left it.

The lawyer's question about "and who is my neighbor?" really means, "Who can I exclude from being my neighbor so that I do not have to love them?" In other words, "What humans are not really human?" This is a dehumanizing question whose answer could be used to justify violence against another group and the violence being done. This question is a key part of the crisis of our times.

Christians understand the Samaritan's willingness to risk for a fellow human being is ideal. We understand the moral of the story but often miss what Jesus is modeling.

Jesus could have told a story about how a Jewish person risked caring for a Samaritan. But this may have strengthened the assumption that Jesus' in-group are the truly human ones. Instead, Jesus flipped the script. He told a story about how a Samaritan had the humanity because of his upbringing and tradition to take a risk for the wellbeing of a person from another in-group, in this case, a Jewish person.

In response to a dehumanizing dynamic, Jesus told a positive story about a dehumanized group. He lifted up the Samaritan as a model for faithfulness and then suggested that everyone emulate his behavior.

But if we stopped there, we would miss a deeper meaning. Jesus is also asking us to emulate Jesus' own behavior to stand up for the humanity of groups being dehumanized. This was risky for him. It probably cost him followers.

Jesus believed in one Creator, who calls us to recognize one another as human. Jesus risked his public status to recognize the humanity of Samaritans when it was in question. Jesus continues to call disciples to do the same for all dehumanized groups.

Because our identity as God's Beloved is safe and secure, we are free to risk our reputations to stand up with and behind groups that are being dehumanized. Jesus invites us to follow him into our common humanity and go and do likewise.

Hey, What About This Verse?

1 Corinthians 10:20

But the sacrifices of pagans are offered to demons, not to God, and I do not want you to be participants with demons.

Reflection

We often take verses about specific situations and apply them to everyone and everything. This misuse of scripture does not respect the writer, the original readers, and the text itself.

The context that Paul was addressing was the situation of Christians living in the Roman Empire. Later in this book, I'll offer a description of the domination culture of the Empire. In short, the Roman Empire believed that to be human is to seek power over other people. Taking other people's property, forcing people into slavery, and oppressing others was considered their divine right. They crucified people who resisted their Empire. Imagine the pain, fear, and suffering people experienced in this Domination culture!

The public religions of Rome supported the Empire's domination culture. They claimed that their culture was of divine origin and operated in divine will. For instance, the Roman Empire promoted the idea that Emperor Augustus was the son of the God Apollo. N. T. Wright writes that "in Paul's time, emperor worship . . . was springing up all round the Roman empire," and shrines were increasingly dedicated to the Roman emperor and his family.[13] In this and other passages, Paul was not saying that all other religions are demonic. He was saying that the imperial religion functioned to support theft, enslavement, and murder by claiming divine approval for the Empire. These specific Roman religions, Paul wrote, were destroying people and functioned in a demonic way. When the divine is no longer a source of hope for a better world, the demon of despair overcomes human beings. This analysis could be applied to any wisdom tradition, including Christian ones, that support unjust systems by claiming divine approval.

Both Peter (Acts 10) and Paul (Romans 2) made explicit statements about people of other traditions. Here is Paul's:

> For it is not the hearers of the law who are righteous
> in God's sight, but the doers of the law who will be
> justified. When Gentiles, who do not possess the law,
> do instinctively what the law requires, these, though
> not having the law, are a law to themselves. They
> show that what the law requires is written on their
> hearts, to which their own conscience also bears
> witness.
> Romans 2:13-15a

Paul reminded the Gentile and Jewish Christians that people in other cultures and traditions love the Creator with all their hearts and love their neighbors as themselves–as on these two core teachings hang the instruction of the Torah and the prophets.

This First Corinthians text and others like it should not be understood to be saying that other traditions are by definition wrong, invalid, or evil. Nor was he proposing that Christians are an exclusive in-group. He was saying that we must not take any part in systems that hurt other beings, a call which includes critiquing our own tradition about whether it spurs us to love our neighbors as ourselves. Every tradition includes reform movements, self-critiques, and those who remember how their tradition has fallen short of their values.

Section Two: Abrahamic Blessing

Key Question: What does our wisdom tradition propose about the diversity of human beings, human communities, and wisdom traditions?

Summary: We live in a connected world in which experiencing differences in cultures and traditions is almost unavoidable. The Abrahamic tradition teaches us about how to relate to different groups, cultures, and traditions. Building on the concept of one Creator and a set of common parents for all human beings, Abraham is called to form an in-group–not an exclusive in-group–but one that honors the value of other in-groups. Humans often compete for status, but there is only one status that matters, according to our tradition: child of God. Sadly, the vision of creating an in-group and tradition that honors the unity in diversity of human beings has been lost for much of Christian history in the Western church. A primary example of this loss of our values is the Doctrines of Discovery.

Chapter Six: Abraham's Call

> Now the Lord said to Abram, "Go from your
> country and your kindred and your father's house
> to the land that I will show you. I will make of you
> a great nation, and I will bless you, and make your
> name great, so that you will be a blessing. I will bless
> those who bless you, and the one who curses you
> I will curse; and in you all the families of the earth
> shall be blessed." So Abram went, as the Lord had
> told him.
> Genesis 12:1-4

Abraham, once known as Abram, was called to start a new tradition, a new in-group, a new clan, a new tribe.

It is a good thing for human beings to have an in-group and tradition. It is not good to be alone. In the days of Abraham, there were no grocery stores, eBay, or Amazon Prime. In Abraham's day, all needs were met by family and clan. The same went for our safety. Our family and clan protected us, and we protected them. In this passage, the Creator invited Abraham to be a part of the Creator's family by saying, "I will bless those who bless you, and the one who curses you I will curse." God's deep purpose is not to curse but to bless. This text includes the sad reality that there are times when we must protect our families against those who wish to do us harm. Of course, this can easily get out of control. In-groups can place their needs over the needs of others or create conflict even when avoidable. How we imagine and manage the needs of our own in-group and those of others is one of the greatest challenges for human beings.

God promised to make Abraham's family great and numerous–but with a purpose. Abraham's new in-group was to be a blessing. The word blessing in Hebrew is brachah. It comes from a root word that means to kneel. To be a blessing has several meanings:

- To speak well of others.
- To offer the best we have to others with humility.

Then comes the last part, in verse three: "In you, all the families of the earth shall be blessed."

The word "families" here is very important. In Hebrew, *mishpachah* means clan, family, tradition, in-group, tribe, species, kind, and nation. This term includes the reality that every clan has its own culture, tradition, language, practical skills, religion, and spirituality.

Abraham was called to create an in-group whose purpose was not just to survive and thrive as a group but to speak well of other groups and to offer the best they had in humility so that all groups could survive and thrive. Abraham's in-group and tradition had core values of recognizing the inherent value of living in cooperation with and respect for other in-groups of diverse cultures or wisdom traditions.

> [This text] links the traditions of God's providential
> care for the world and God's electing call of Israel.[14]
> Walter Brueggemann

To counter the human tendency to see people of other traditions and in-groups as not fully human, Abraham was called to actively work for the good of other in-groups in recognition of our common humanity. We are called to love our neighbor as we love ourselves. Our collective needs must be considered when we are meeting our own. Ultimately, we can only thrive when we all thrive.

This does not mean that the children of Abraham are uniquely responsible for other families. Many Christians assume this is true, placing undue responsibility on Jewish people and, at the same time, claiming we know what is best for others. The text does not say this. Rather, it is saying that the Creator will bless all families through Abraham's children. A key part of this blessing comes from God's call to create an in-group that recognized other in-groups as human. All the *mishpachah* are blessed when we all see each other as human and help each other thrive.

> The wellbeing of Israel carried potential for the
> wellbeing of other nations. Israel is never permitted
> to live in a vacuum. It must always live with, for,
> and among others.[15]
> Walter Brueggemann

Christians, being one of the Abrahamic traditions, would do well to remember that this applies to us as well.

Some historians say that the society in Ur was having trouble respecting other in-groups and traditions in Abraham's time.[16] It wasn't always that way. Yet, at that time, their storytellers and leaders were offering divine affirmation to enslave people from other groups. This is not okay–then, now, or ever.

Any wisdom tradition can be twisted to offer divine affirmation to support injustice. There were many things about the wisdom traditions from Mesopotamia that we would recognize as important, ethical teachings. But Abraham was called to respond to his time's instance of twisted teaching that supported exclusive in-grouping and dehumanization.

Abraham was called to create an in-group that would:

- recognize other in-groups as human, made in God's image
- speak well of all in-groups
- cooperate in humility with them by offering their best to others

Lessons for Today

There are two big issues taking place in our world and in the United States. Due to contextual factors like political rhetoric, income inequality, racist policies and ideas, historical trauma, and social media, we are seeing the rise of two primary dynamics:

- **Exclusive In-Grouping:** The assumption that the only valid group is our own.
- **Dehumanization:** A process in which other in-groups are seen as less than human, thus appropriate targets of violence.

Taken together, these trends threaten the functioning and future of our democracy and the peace of our communities.

Paths to Understanding's effort, Let's Go Together, is an attempt to counter exclusive in-grouping and dehumanization. There are other such efforts across the nation and the world.[17] What we have realized is that our ancient wisdom traditions propose a strategy for how we can deal with the challenges of our day. Wisdom traditions often emerge in a time of crisis when human community is endangered. They grow and are remembered because they carry ancient wisdom about how we can live together and thrive together.

Wisdom traditions invite us to name our issues and understand human vulnerabilities. They offer powerful, sustainable, and replicable strategies to bring out the best in us and help us through our own time of challenges.

We can see exclusive in-grouping at work all around us. We see people in many wisdom traditions saying that only they have the answers and only they are fully human. We also see this across ideological and political lines. People feel so estranged and divided from each other that family members have stopped talking, groups are suspicious of each other, and many people are isolated, almost segregated from their neighbors. Churches and service clubs lack diversity, siloed in sameness.

This didn't just happen. Some leaders and influencers understand what human beings are vulnerable to. They know how to separate us. They know we are vulnerable to in-group bias that can grow into fear of, hatred for, and violence toward other human beings. They build on the historic exclusive in-grouping of racism, sexism, and so on. They know that once we start this cycle, we create real grievances with each other. Then retribution starts and self-perpetuates like fire. As I said earlier, approximately 4 percent of Americans report that they are ready to engage in political violence to save the country. That's about 12 million people.[18]

These dividers are using a process called dehumanization to make us believe that the other in-groups are not really human or are such a threat that we can't respect their humanity. The process goes like this:

- influential people propose an "Us vs. Them"
- they say that "those people" aren't human
- leaders begin to collectively blame the "them"
- the same people suggest a threat (the fear this inspires is real, even when the threat is not)
- then there seems to be no alternative
- the conclusion is that violence is necessary/good
- and a peaceful future awaits - if we act with violence now

These dividers are often using differences in wisdom, tradition, political ideology, culture, skin color, and our geography (urban, rural, etc.) to divide us. Groups in this nation spend millions of dollars each year to divide Americans from one another.

In her book, *The Age of Mega-Identity Politics*, Liliana Mason shows how we became divided into "Pottery Barn, Latte loving" and "Crackerbarrel, Chick-fil-A" in-groups. Increasingly, the two sides don't see each other as human. People don't want to marry someone from the "other side" and are sorting themselves into different regions. A neighbor of mine moved recently. He and his wife wanted to live in a location where people agreed with what he considered family values. He looked at me as if I had no values.

These kinds of divisions, when they reach the level of exclusive in-grouping and dehumanization, lead to violence.

These dividers use this dehumanization process to make us more fearful of and isolated from one another. This increases the conditions in which people join hate groups who form an exclusive in-group explicitly dedicated to dehumanization of and violence toward targeted groups

Response to Dehumanization

In the last century, over two-hundred-and-sixty million people were killed in genocides.[19] Most of the people who participated in the killing or sat by in silence did not do so because they wanted to be part of evil acts. They were so infected by ideas of dehumanization, built upon an in-group bias turned toxic, that they felt it was morally right to do or allow violence against another group.

While genocide is the act of a nation, hate groups seek to engage in this kind of violence on their own. Members of hate groups are the bulk of those who are ready to engage in political violence. We have seen this political violence at work. I have seen it first-hand against people of diverse races, religions, and cultures.

But this next point is important. Dehumanization doesn't just happen in other people. It is at work in us. It is at work in me.

Instead of encouraging this process of dehumanization, Abraham's call in Genesis 12 is a direct attempt to create an in-group that would:

- resist the toxicity of exclusive in-grouping by recognizing others as human
- respond to dehumanization by speaking well of and working for the wellbeing of other in-groups

Abraham's call is not just some flowery words spoken long

ago and written in a scripture. Abraham's call contains a strategy for what we can do when neighborhoods and societies are falling apart. Abraham's children, then, have been given a strategy to meet this moment.

We can build trust in one another when we know each other, do good with and for each other, and show respect to each other by associating in public together. Communities of wisdom must understand human nature as well as the dividers do. We must be more committed and organized to bring people together than the hate groups are to harming others.

As we go forward, I will show how Jesus of Nazareth was faithful in his own time to the call of Abraham.

- It is good to have a tradition because they enable us to learn from the wisdom of our ancestors.
- It is good to have an in-group because they provide support, companionship, and, ideally, challenge.

Abraham was called to begin a community so that we could receive both of these gifts. This group was called to counter their own tendency toward exclusive in-grouping with the core value of honoring, blessing, and working for the common good with other traditions, cultures, and in-groups. We are in this together.

Our question is: Will we answer the call of Abraham in our time as Jesus did? Will we go and do likewise?

Chapter Seven: Pluralism

I was teaching in a church about the danger of dehumanization of Muslims and many other groups. The building displayed many crosses. I was wearing a clergy collar. A woman with a cross around her neck said, "Well, I don't mind Muslims, but if they are to be here, they should not wear that head thing."

She was talking about the hijab. I then took my clergy collar off and threw it on the ground. I asked, "Are you suggesting that we institute a dress code in the United States? If so, who gets to decide what we get to wear?" There was an oil painting on the wall. It showed Mary with Jesus on her lap. She was wearing a hijab, as most any Mediterranean woman would wear in her time and to this day. I asked the group to consider what Mary was wearing. Should we ban paintings of Mary with her head covered?

Her deeper questions were:

- Does God intend us to have one culture and one wisdom tradition?
- Are we a mono-cultural nation or a pluralist nation?

Pluralism in the Abrahamic Tradition

One Creator means that there is a unity in the creation. But unity is not synonymous with sameness. The creation is made of a multitude of different galaxies, stars, planets, animals, plants, and people. Monotheism includes unity and diversity. Our bodies are made of many types of cells with the same DNA but with diverse functions that make our lives possible.

If God intended there to be one tradition, Abraham's call would have been quite different from what it was. God would have told Abraham to convert or kill other in-groups until everyone was blessed by the creation of a monoculture: one tradition, one language, one ring to rule them all.

Monotheism often includes one set of parents for all the peoples, clans, and traditions and one Creator that holds them all in love.

Abraham's call was to be a blessing to all the other in-groups: to both speak well of others and offer our best in humility for the mutual thriving of all. Rabbi Levine and Father Treacy, the original founders of Paths to Understanding, worked for unity in the human family–a family comprised of people from all wisdom, traditions, and cultures. Rabbi Levine shared how important this is for all the human family.

> We, as a human race, are inextricably
> interdependent. We need each other if we're going
> to survive. Therefore, [Brotherhood] is not merely
> a pious platitude. It's the very condition of human
> survival on this planet.
> Rabbi Levine

Rabbi Levine was clear that the Abrahamic tradition is what we call a pluralist tradition: that there are numerous distinct ethnic, religious, and cultural groups that together form our understanding of who "we" are as a people.

Abrahamic in-groups have engaged in exclusive in-grouping, dehumanization, and violence towards others many times. I'll address this later. Conflicts emerge between in-groups. It is okay to protect our in-group when needed, but the ideals of the Abrahamic tradition are deeply pluralistic. It is a blessing to have a tradition and a tribe. Still, the core values of our in-group include recognizing the humanity, upholding the dignity, and living in respect for other traditions and tribes. It is important to be clear about our values, even when we fall short of them.

Pluralism in America

E pluribus Unum, a Latin phrase meaning "out of many, one," was the motto of the United States chosen by Adams, Jefferson, and Franklin. The pluralistic vision of the Abrahamic tradition was acknowledged among some of the founding mothers and fathers of our nation. But only partially, as we take into account the denial of human rights to women, indigenous people, and enslaved people forcibly taken from Africa.

Abigail Adams, wife of the second President of the United States of America, wrote:

> The Universal Parent has dispensed his blessings
> throughout all creation . . . Though seas, mountains,
> and rivers are geographical boundaries, they
> contract not the benevolence and the good will of
> the liberal mind, which can extend itself beyond the
> limits of country and kindred, and claim fellowship
> with Christian, Jew, or Turk. What a lesson, did the
> great Author of our religion give to mankind by the
> parable of the Jew and the Samaritan; but how little
> it has been regarded![20]
> Abigail Adams

Her vision included people of all traditions. The many are part of the one, but they don't lose what makes them distinct and unique. Thomas Jefferson's vision of religious freedom included wisdom traditions from around the world, along with those who decide not to be part of one:

As he wrote in surviving fragments of his autobiography, Thomas Jefferson intended his *Virginia Statute of Religious Freedom* to protect "the Jew and the Gentile, the Christian and Mahometan, the Hindoo, and infidel of every denomination."[21]

This *Statute of Religious Freedom* in Virginia informed the First Amendment to the US Constitution, which reads:

> Congress shall make no law respecting an
> establishment of religion or prohibiting the free
> exercise thereof.

Human rights are not a limited good. To defend the rights of some is to defend the rights of all.

The founders did not try to provide a once and for all list of rights. They were wise enough to know that they did not have the wisdom to name them all. In the Declaration of Independence, they wrote:

> We hold these truths to be self-evident, that all [men]
> are created equal, that they are endowed by their
> Creator with certain unalienable Rights, that among
> these are Life, Liberty, and the pursuit of Happiness.

These are only a short beginning of a much longer list of human rights. Sadly, when they wrote "men," they literally meant property-holding, white men. Yet the wisdom of their words in-spired our nation to expand the definition of "men" to include many more humans than they foresaw. Of course, the founders knew this would happen. They wrote:

> We the people of the United States of America, in
> order to form a more perfect union...

They didn't claim it was going to be perfect. The deepest form of patriotism is to recognize the ways we fall short of a perfect union and to take steps to make it better. The US constitution is a set of aspirational values as well as the basis for our laws. True patrio-tism includes aspiring to live these aspirational values more fully. True patriotism includes protecting the rights of others.

America's aspirational constitutional values include the freedom to belong, or not belong, to any wisdom tradition. It is fundamen-tally a pluralistic vision: out of many, we become one. How we envision the "one" is very important. There are three main ways America has understood being one:

- exclusion–only one group of people can be fully American
- assimilation–only one legitimate culture can be expressed in America
- pluralism–America is ideally people of diverse cultures agreeing to constitutional values and participation in our constitutional republic

> For the pluralists, like Horace Kallen in the early
> twentieth century, the American promise was to
> come as you are, with all your differences and
> angularities, pledged only to the common civic
> demands of American citizenship. Come and be
> yourself, contributing in your distinctive way to the
> "orchestra" of American civilization.[22]
> Diana Eck

The pluralism in wisdom traditions and in the United States is never perfect. Some people in these groups focus their energies on exclusive in-grouping and dehumanization of others. This always leads to violence of some kind and means that the struggle for plu-ralism is never finished. As Jesus said, "Blessed are the peacemak-ers."

Implications of Pluralism

Diana Eck, the Director of The Pluralism Project at Harvard, has proposed four implications of Pluralism:

- First, pluralism is not diversity alone but the energetic engagement with diversity. Diversity can and has meant the creation of religious ghettoes with little traffic between or among them. Today, religious diversity is a given, but pluralism is not a given; it is an achievement. Mere diversity without real encounters and relationships will yield increasing tensions in our societies.
- Second, pluralism is not just tolerance, but the active seeking of understanding across lines of difference. . . It [tolerance] does nothing to remove our ignorance of one another and leaves in place the stereotype, the half-truth, the fears that underlie old patterns of division and violence.
- Third, pluralism is not relativism but the encounter of commitments. The new paradigm of pluralism does not require us to leave our identities and our commitments behind, for pluralism is the encounter of commitments. It means holding our deepest differences, even our religious differences, not in isolation but in relationship to one another.
- Fourth, pluralism in America is clearly based on the common ground rules of the First Amendment to the Constitution: "no establishment" of religion and the "free exercise" of religion.

You can read more of her work in the resources on our website. These are beautiful. I add two of my own for emphasis as exclusive in-grouping and dehumanization endanger the functioning of our society:

- Fifth, pluralism means that we work together for the common good across all lines of difference.
- Sixth, pluralism means that we relate to one another in public on the basis of our common values, even while we may compete in the public square about values in which we differ.

Communities of wisdom have a right to practice their traditions and cultures, a right that is affirmed both in the Abrahamic traditions and our Constitutional framework. Communities of wisdom also have a responsibility to each other at this moment so that we make sure everyone is able to exercise their right.

Wisdom traditions are powerful. Today, we need to understand the nature of that power. In this time of exclusive in-grouping and dehumanization, we can make a difference. When we build relationships, work for the common good, and show up in public spaces together in mutual respect, we can help rebuild our trust in each other for a brighter future.

We need each other.

We are better together.

Chapter Eight: Proposing Modesty

One of the ways that exclusive in-grouping is expressed is when people in a wisdom tradition think that they understand the truth for all time and that others don't. I have heard such among people of all wisdom traditions–and those who don't have one. But each tradition warns people about the limits of human understanding and the limits of the tradition itself.

Our Story About Our Family

We often trade stories with friends about our families, where we grew up, and our early life experiences. Storytelling helps us to understand each other. Many of us can go on for hours telling funny stories, explaining strange habits, and talking about the loving ways of our families.

> The universe is made of stories, not atoms.
> Muriel Rukeyser

Her point isn't that atoms don't exist. Rather, she is pointing out that we order our lives by our stories. Even our thoughts about atoms get arranged into stories!

As a young adult, I shared with my friends how much I appreciated how resilient and stubborn my Mother was in the face of her disease. One day, my friends came home with me. Over dinner, I told my friends, in front of my Mother, how much I appreciated her resilience and stubborn response. I was giving her credit.

But she saw it differently. She said, "I didn't do that to be stubborn. I did it because I wanted to take care of my family."

I realized in that moment that she was bigger, more mysterious, and complex than I realized. I had experiences of her, but could I really claim to have her figured out? I think not. Here, Paul reminds us that we are not mind readers–of others or of God.

> For what human being knows what is truly human
> except the human spirit that is within? So also, no
> one comprehends what is truly God's except the
> Spirit of God.
> 1 Corinthians 2:11

When we are in someone's presence, we are invited to see them as a person, a presence, a human, a mystery that our words cannot contain. Out of respect for them, we are invited to a certain **modesty of speech** about them. Their story is their story. All of us want to be able to tell our own story and not have others reduce us to their vision of us. How would you feel if someone told **your story** around the table? I have had people try to tell my story. I felt disrespected, unseen, and invalidated.

Respect for my Mother included recognizing that she was more than I knew. Our stories about our families are holy, whether painful or beautiful. These stories help us to see our universe and ourselves in it. But stories have limits.

Stories about Life

In our wisdom traditions, we tell stories, make art, craft poetry, participate in rituals, and reflect on the meaning and mystery of life. We strive to express what is common between all of us and unique to each one of us. Every wisdom tradition encourages modesty as we reflect on God, the Divine, and life. God's story is God's story–not ours.

The Hebrew Scripture tells us that Moses saw a bush that was burning but not consumed. The voice gave a name and not a name: I AM who I AM. With this intentionally mysterious Divine name, Moses accepted the call to go to Egypt and take on a difficult task. Later, Moses goes to the top of Mount Sinai. He does not see God but rather the brightness of God in the clouds. Moses' face radiated with that light. But still, he did not see God. Elijah, too, wanted to see the Creator but experienced a wind and an earthquake–and God was not in either. Then he heard a still, small voice.

The Christian Scriptures speak of Jesus as the embodiment of God. No one has ever seen God, but for Christians, Jesus reveals God. He is the Word made flesh. The word "logos" here means something like "the Divine wisdom" that holds all things together and through whom all is made. The story of Jesus invites us to see that God is committed to loving, healing, and creating the world. Jesus does so by becoming a part of it, enjoying life, suffering with and for it, and bringing new life to it.

We Christians say a LOT of things, sing a lot of songs, and write a lot of theology about Jesus. But again, imagine how we would feel if Jesus was sitting with us and listening in? We might want to listen more than speak. We might be just a bit more modest as we would when our mother is in the room. Of course, Christians believe that Jesus is in the room.

Jesus himself spoke to the untameable mystery of the Spirit–the Divine Presence in the world.

> The wind blows where it chooses, and you hear the
> sound of it, but you do not know where it comes
> from or where it goes. So it is with everyone who is
> born of the Spirit.
> John 3:8

God is beyond our knowing and our control–God is free to surprise us. We don't own God.

Paul encourages us all to modesty about the mystery of the Divine:

> For now, we see in a mirror dimly, but then we will
> see face to face. Now I know only in part; then I will
> know fully, even as I have been fully known.
> 1 Corinthians 13:12

In Jesus, God is revealed to Christians, but that doesn't mean we possess or can define God or Jesus. Just because the Holy Wind blew in forming the Christian community doesn't mean the Wind has stopped blowing where She will. God is in, with, and under us. This theme of respecting the mystery of God continued through the early centuries of Christianity. Gregory of Nyssa, a highly influential Christian thinker, said:

> Following the instructions of the Holy Scripture, we
> have been taught that the nature of God is beyond
> human speech.[23]
> Gregory of Nyssa

Like Moses, Elijah, Paul, and so many others, we can both be modest about what we say about God and be faithful to our calling. Our respect leads both to modesty about what we say **about** God and to risking ourselves to bold ventures in faithfulness **to** God. Respect for my Mother meant modesty in what I claimed about her but make no mistake: When she asked me to do something, I did it.

When we become so certain of our view of God, we can close ourselves off from learning more and acting out of love. Jesus pointed out this universal human tendency when he quoted his own people's words of self-critique about "stoning the prophets."

Living in a Multi-Storied World

There are literally thousands of different wisdom traditions in the world. *In-group bias* is the term we use to name our tendency to think that our group is the best and that other in-groups are not as valid. We are all vulnerable to this. Similarly, *confirmation bias* is the name for our tendency to hear and believe information or stories about others that support our views and to reject what does not.

Many Christians who proclaim their faith in God are actually using God language and the Christian Scriptures as a tool of confirmation bias. When we do this, we only honor what supports our view and disregard what challenges us. When we do this, we are rejecting the Creator's love and the Creator's call to change, to become more fully who we are made to be.

Encountering people of diverse traditions and cultures, we find much in common and notice some important differences. They, too, have mothers and fathers and family to tell stories about. They, too, have stories about life and how we can live it together.

We live in a multi-story universe, and there are many wisdom traditions in the world. How do we relate to them? Kathryn Lohre, Executive for Ecumenical and Inter-Religious Relations & Theological Discernment of the Evangelical Lutheran Church of America, shared this response to the question of how to relate to other traditions:

> Kathyrn Lohre: People have the wrong idea about what interfaith actually is, and they're deeply concerned that in order to participate in it or engage with people of other religions and worldviews, they have to give something up, they have to compromise who they are, they have to set aside their beliefs or their convictions in order to, you know, reach some sort of lowest common denominator. And that, of

course, I think is not what any of us here or in our networks mean by interfaith or inter-religious work.

One of my mentors in this work is my former professor, Diana Eck, and I worked with her for many years at the pluralism project. I really appreciate that she disrupted this by providing people with very simple language of engagement, that religious pluralism, in her definition, is about engaging people across difference and not forsaking who we are or setting aside our convictions. It's that two-way street that I think all of us have experienced in our lives and in our work, where you enter into inter-religious relations. You don't set aside or give up anything, but you actually gain something, both in terms of what you learn about your neighbor but also what you learn about yourself. I can say I've learned much more about what it means to be a Christian in the Lutheran tradition through inter-religious relations than I did through the excellent catechesis information I received growing up because you have to learn to articulate what your beliefs and convictions are to your neighbor in a way that helps everyone at the table understand what both the common similarities are and the common convictions but also where those important differences are.

Kathryn emphasizes that we relate to other traditions by engaging authentically with them around our similarities and our differences.[24] Instead of requiring us to give up who we are, this process helps us to respect our neighbors more fully along with gaining a better understanding of our own convictions.

Chapter Nine: Diminishing Status

I experienced a status keeping system in my hometown. Chances are you have, too. I have come to see that Jesus invited us out of the competition that such systems create. He wanted to create the possibility for cooperation between people and between in-groups who were part of different levels of the status system. In his community, he wanted to give an example of another way to live where status did not determine the worth of each human being.

> Jesus called them and said to them, "You know that among the Gentiles those whom they recognize as their rulers lord it over them, and their great ones are tyrants over them. But it is not so among you; but whoever wishes to become great among you must be your servant, and whoever wishes to be first among you must be servant of all. For the Son of Man came not to be served but to serve, and to give his life a ransom for many."
> Mark 10:42-45

God's Dream in a Roman Nightmare

In this passage, Jesus was working to help his disciples understand the nature of the community he was creating. James and John had asked to sit on his right and left–to be high officials in the new government Jesus was going to Jerusalem to install. But Jesus offers another way. In his community, in contrast to the Roman culture around and in them, they would seek to remain in a mutual relationship by serving each other.

Now, let's be perfectly clear: The shape of this new community was not new. This kind of community was taught before through the teaching of

- belief in One Creator
- humans made in God's image
- Abraham's call to be a blessing to all nations
- loving your neighbor as you love yourself
- God freeing enslaved people from Egypt

Jesus was a leader in the Abrahamic tradition. He was leading people in his day to the Abrahamic understanding of God's vision and dream for how human beings can live together. He led people toward this vision within the context of Roman occupation.

The Roman culture was a domination culture: The more powerful someone was, the more fully human they were perceived to be. Therefore, for someone to love their family, they needed to dominate other people. When they could not dominate others themselves, they would submit themselves to powerful others with whom they could dominate others.

Because of the Roman domination culture in Jesus' day, people were constantly engaged in a competition for status. Status determined who your family could marry, with whom you could trade, and your chances of survival. They were living in a caste system that determined who was important and who was not, who was blessed and who was not. The family you were born into determined your opportunities in life. This is why Jesus is often identified as the son of Mary and being born in Nazareth. 'Son of Mary' meant that he was born in less than acceptable circumstances, conceived outside of marriage, 'born in sin.' It also served as a put down as most people were referred to as son of their father. He was also from an unimportant town–people in that day used to say that nothing good could come out of Nazareth. When Jesus was baptized, he stepped out of the status-keeping system. He died to his birthplace in that status-keeping system when he arose from the waters of the Jordan.

In her book, *Caste*, Isabel Wilkerson helps us to understand what a caste[25] system is:

> Caste is the granting or withholding of respect,
> status, honor, attention, privileges, resources, benefit
> of the doubt, and human kindness to someone on
> the basis of their perceived rank or standing in the
> hierarchy.
> Isabel Wilkerson

A caste system set the tone for human relationships in Jesus' day and our own.[26]

Swimming in the cultural waters of a caste system, Jesus' disciples thought Jesus was going to Jerusalem to replace those in power. But Jesus was not seeking to replace those in power. He was seeking to change the very notion of what power is. He was not seeking to win the game but to change the game.

When Jesus announced God's reign, he was saying that God was once again calling for another way for human beings to understand themselves and to live with one another. Instead of the **Kingdom of Rome**, he proposed the **Kindom of God**. We will discuss more about the Kindom of God as we go.

Our humanity is not derived from how we rank. **The only status that matters is that we all are made in God's image.** We may play different roles in the community, but we are all equal in status before God and one another.

Caste systems diminish human beings. Caste denies:

- everyone's inherent worth and dignity
- experience of true community with each other, turning us into gladiators instead of partners
- our capacity for generosity, compassion, and reconciliation as we assume that people "get what they deserve"
- our common, intertwined future

When we live in a caste system, we can lose touch with our own humanity because we lose touch with one another's humanity. In response to the disciples, Jesus was clear: It shall not be so among you. Because of this change in the understanding of status, Jesus' community began to call each other siblings. They became a part of a new family. This is why I am using the term "Kindom" to express Jesus' "Kingdom of God." Where "Kingdom" stresses one ruler at the top of a status system, the word "kindom" emphasizes that there is no hierarchical status system in the community because we are all kin, children of God.

The Roman Empire knew exactly how powerful recognizing our common humanity was. That is why they killed Jesus and others like him.

In Jesus, we see a powerful re-imagination not only of how humans can live with each other but of how God engages with humans. This re-imagination is important because God-language is always aspirational:

- We desire to become like the God we imagine.
- We create communities based on the God we imagine.
- We create our idea of "god" to justify our society.

The character of God we see revealed in Jesus is One who is not only "all powerful" but also who is vulnerable–a God who bleeds, suffers, and dies. In Jesus, the Son of God, we see what God is like, we see what God would do, and we see how God acts in the world. God does not seek to have power over us but rather respects human freedom to respond. God risks Godself to be reconciled with us and to reconcile us to each other.

Jesus is described not only as the Son of God but also as the fully human one. The kind of human being re-imagined by this God who risks Godself is a human who embraces both our potential and our vulnerability, our power and our weakness, our life and our eventual death. This vision of the human, in stark contrast to the Roman ideal, knows that we can do many things but does not despise our limits as something that makes us sub-human. Because we are embraced in our full humanity, we can begin to embrace our own lives.

This vision is also in stark contrast to the reality of life in the United States. Some of our ideals speak of "We the people" and "liberty and justice for all." This is good. Yet, from the founding of the nation, we have consistently decided that some people are not fully human. We have made some progress in being more true to these ideals: changing laws and policies toward a more perfect union. Yet, we remain more in competition against each other than in partnership with each other.

In the Kindom of God, we seek partnership with others, respecting both the limits and the capacities of each. God calls us **power with each other**, not over each other. God calls us into a community of partnership and mutuality because, by sheer gift, God seeks to have power with us.

Let the Children Come

This disoriented the disciples. It disorients us. But being disoriented is a part of the disciple-of-Jesus gig.

> People were bringing little children to him in order
> that he might touch them; and the disciples spoke

sternly to them. But when Jesus saw this, he was
indignant and said to them, "Let the little children
come to me; do not stop them; for it is to such as
these that the kingdom of God belongs. Truly I tell
you, whoever does not receive the kingdom of God
as a little child will never enter it." And he took
them up in his arms, laid his hands on them, and
blessed them.
Mark 10:13-16

In the 1st century, children had no status or honor rating until
they became twelve. Your status was determined by the status of
your family, but you could lose status by hanging out in public
with lower status people. This was dangerous, literally. Your status determined who would help you, trade with you, and partner
with you. Your family could be economically vulnerable if you
lost your status. So, when Jesus took the child into his arms, he
symbolically gave up his status. He was saying that participation
in the Kindom of God required giving up the caste system. Jesus
was saying that he no longer wanted to play the status game as his
culture played it. Jesus was saying that to be a disciple is to give
up status games and strive for a community of mutuality. Baptism
means to die to caste.

Jesus doesn't give a hoot about his status in the caste system.
He shows this in who he eats with, who he speaks to, and who he
heals.

Now all the tax collectors and sinners were coming
near to listen to him. And the Pharisees and the
scribes were grumbling and saying, "This fellow
welcomes sinners and eats with them."
Luke 15:1-2

Yes, he did! Jesus welcomed and ate with Samaritans, Syrophoe-
nicians, Canaanites, Romans, lepers, women, children and on and
on. The only status that mattered to Jesus is one we all share: Children of One Creator who loves, respects, and values each of us.

We Are All Children

Our common status of Children of God leads us out of the caste
system within our own churchy in-group:

Be of the same mind, having the same love, being in

full accord and of one mind. Do nothing from selfish
ambition or conceit, but in humility regard others as
better than yourselves. Let each of you look not to
your own interests, but to the interests of others. Let
the same mind be in you that was in Christ Jesus,
who, though he was in the form of God,
did not regard equality with God
as something to be exploited,
but emptied himself,
taking the form of a slave,
being born in human likeness.[27]
Philippians 2:2-7

Jesus' leadership did not simply propose by example that we act
differently in our own in-group but also toward other in-groups.
This is why his caste-system-breaking behavior included welcoming people outside his own group.

I have other sheep that do not belong to this fold.
I must bring them also, and they will listen to my
voice. So there will be one flock, one shepherd.
John 10:16

As Peter engaged with people of diverse traditions, he began to
be reoriented.

Then Peter began to speak to them: 'I truly
understand that God shows no partiality, but in
every nation anyone who fears him and does what is
right is acceptable to him.
Acts 10:34-35

God honors people of all *mishpachah*s. Jesus' leadership grew from
the Abrahamic tradition. He honored the dignity of people outside
his in-group because he believed that the one Creator intended the
unity and diversity of human beings and human communities. The
true inheritance of all of Abraham's children is recognizing the status of all human beings as God's children. Part of the dying and
rising of baptism is to give up our status within the caste system. In
doing so, we lose our public identity in the caste system. In doing
so, we recognize the one status that matters: Child of God among
all our siblings.

But this leads to a challenging question: Are we, like Jesus, willing to risk our status to relate to all of God's children?

Father William Treacy believed that the power of compassion, through person-to-person relationships, is central to our seeing each other as human—and that it is worth it even when it is risky.

> Father William Treacy: First of all, I'm impressed by my colleagues talking about the importance of getting to know people. . .
>
> A priest who was a medic in the Nazi army in Russia was bringing back some severely wounded German soldiers. He came to a Russian farmhouse, and he had to get them in out of the freezing cold. So, he knocked on the door and asked, could they shelter these two German soldiers? Well, they were very hesitant because if the word got out, their life would be taken. Finally, they agreed to take them. He said, "just give them water." In the morning, when he went to get them, he found this Russian couple had stayed up all night and made soup for the German soldiers. Well, he was quite taken by this. "I didn't ask you to do that," he said. The woman spoke up and said, "I have a son in the Russian army fighting on the German front. If he was this injured in Germany, I believe a German mother would care for him."
>
> So, compassion, meeting face-to-face, turned her from being anti-German, anti-Nazi, into showing compassion for them. That's why I agree with my colleagues that getting to know one another as people, getting to know you [Aneelah]. I mean, just your background, your family, and so on, changes my attitude. It's not an intellectual thing, but it's a person-to-person [thing].

We are all children. We have no status that we need to protect, no power games we need to play, no status seeking we need to do in which we see each other only as competitors. We are all children of the One. We are both free and called to honor the dignity of every person and every tradition, culture, and group—even when it is risky within a caste system.

As we face our challenges both in local communities and around the world, Jesus calls us to join him in dying to the status-keeping systems that diminish each of us and our common humanity. Imagine us facing our challenges together with the strength, imagination, and joy of diverse wisdom traditions and cultures.

Chapter Ten: Doctrines of Discovery

Jesus grew up in a faithful Jewish household in Nazareth in Galilee. He learned scriptures, memorized Psalms, and debated how
to apply their teachings under occupation by the Roman Empire.
Much of this learning was on his mother's lap.

When the Gospels were written, the writers assumed that the
culture would not change very fast. They told Jesus' story assum-
ing, quite understandably, that the readers would understand all
the references to the Hebrew scripture, the culture, and the politics.
Historian Jaroslav Pelikan writes that *by the end of the first century,
the Jewish context of the gospel writings had been largely forgotten and
that had the most far-reaching consequences on Christian teachings.*[28]

In the year 67, a Jewish revolt cast the Romans from Jerusalem.
Then, in the year 70, the Roman army came back, destroyed the
Temple, and forbade Jews to live near Jerusalem.

As Christians began to focus more on creating community with
Gentile groups, they began to lose the cultural information necessary to understand the Gospels fully. One simple example of this
loss of cultural understanding is the term "eye of a needle." Jesus teaches that the rich must "go through the eye of a needle" to
participate in the Kindom of God. Our minds envision a needle
and thread and so assume that the rich simply cannot enter. But
the "eye of a needle" was a small gate through which a trader's
camel could enter, but only on its knees after all possessions were
removed. After the camel entered this small gate, then it could be
loaded up again. Jesus seems to be speaking of a baptismal transformation for those of us who find our identity in our possessions.

The Roman Empire disrupted the culture and wisdom tradition
of our Jewish neighbors. It also led to memory loss among Christians about the 1st century culture of Judea and the Hebrew Tradition. This loss of the context of Jesus' leadership made it easy to

twist his leadership and lose the wisdom of his teaching and the wisdom of his community.

A Brief Word about Domination

A word about the term "domination culture" is in order here. Cultures can orient themselves to mutuality or to domination. Societies often move back and forth, emphasizing one and then the other.

All cultures have beauty and worth. I believe that Jesus leads us to work for cultures that strive for mutuality. His critique was not about leading us to reduce all cultures to one. Rather he was critiquing the ways that any culture can be vulnerable and oriented to domination. Jesus' leadership encourages us to strive for mutuality in whatever culture we are a part of. In this book, a domination culture is one that is predominantly oriented to domination.

This should in no way suggest that everything about Roman culture is bad. Every culture has beauty because each is a creative expression of the shared life of a group of God's children. Calling a culture a "domination culture" is a critique of its orientation, saying that the primary orientation of that culture is to power over others, competing for status, reducing life to wealth, enslaving or oppressing other people, using the earth as a resource and rejecting its inherent goodness.

In this Sign You Will Conquer

Christianity grew in the first three centuries in Southern and Western Europe. Historian Rodney Stark proposes that it grew largely because Christians took care of each other and shared food with those in their neighborhood.[29] They created a family of equals to bring healing to a culture of domination and status competition.

The 4th century emperor Constantine's mother was Christian. Constantine reported that he saw a vision in the midst of a battle. He saw a cross in the sky and heard a voice from heaven: "In this sign you will conquer." He eventually made Christianity the official religion of the Empire. When his armies would defeat another army, he would force them to be baptized. Then, he would have them killed–but at least they would go to heaven. This made the Creator and the tradition of Jesus into an accessory to murder.

The empire was not converted to anything the Apostles would have recognized as faithful to Jesus' vision. Instead, Christianity was twisted to become a tool of a domination culture. Monotheism was turned into mono-religionism. One humanity was turned into one culture, one government. The Kindom of God in the world was turned into what N.T. Wright has called "postmortem salvation" life after death instead of the Kindom on Earth. God's healing of the world turned into an afterlife insurance policy. Jesus' rejection of violence and coercion was turned into an excuse for domination, murder, and theft. Western Christianity was itself converted to serve the very empire whose way Jesus rejected and sought to change.

It didn't take much to turn a beautiful tradition into a tool of power.

Theologian Douglas John Hall, acknowledging all of this, says that a "thin tradition" remained, a smaller subset of Christians striving to be faithful to God's vision, to the Kindom of God. Not all was lost.

Crusades

The Way of Jesus was converted to offer divine blessing for a domination culture instead of being a blessing for all in-groups. By the time of Charlemagne, the Western Church said that the emperor had "the divine right of kings" to be in power over others. This was another example of the powerful asking for and getting divine sanction from religious leaders.

A few centuries later, Pope Urban II tried to unite Europeans to conquer the Seljuk Turks, Muslims who governed the Holy Land, starting the first of many Christian Crusades. He called for an army to:

> "Enter upon the road to the Holy Sepulcher; wrest that land from the wicked race, and subject it to yourselves ... God has conferred upon you above all nations great glory in arms. Accordingly undertake this journey for the remission of your sins, with the assurance of the imperishable glory of the Kingdom of Heaven.
>
> One witness wrote: "He so influenced to one purpose the desires of all who were present, that they cried out "It is the will of God! It is the will of God!" Urban II replied: "Most beloved brethren, today is manifest in you what the Lord says in the

Gospel, 'Where two or three are gathered together in
my name there am I in the midst of them.'"[30]

Jesus used the idea of "a gathering of two or three" to witness
the power of God in a small group in a domination culture. Now, it
was being used by the domination culture to justify killing people
and taking land. Forgiveness of sins, a promise for a new beginning
with each other, and God was now an invitation to war crimes. The
will of God was no longer something to be sought with awe and
trembling but assumed to agree with our will. The Holy One was
wrongly used as justification for brutal wars against God's very
own holy ones.

Discovering Other People and Their Stuff

In the 15th century, the Moors held quite a lot of territory in mod-
ern-day Spain. The Moors are among my ancestors. These Muslims led what was a very egalitarian society, with thriving Jewish
and Christian communities within their land.

Some Christian rulers, building on Constantine, Charlemagne,
and the Crusades, asked for the Pope to offer divine blessing for a
war to conquer the Moors, here called the Saracens. Here is what
Pope Nicholas the V wrote:

> We grant you by these present documents, with
> our Apostolic Authority, full and free permission
> to invade, search out, capture, and subjugate the
> Saracens and pagans and any other unbelievers and
> enemies of Christ wherever they may be, as well as
> their kingdoms, duchies, counties, principalities, and
> other property [...] and to reduce their persons into
> perpetual servitude.[31]

Just take a moment and consider this. The Abrahamic tradition
and the teachings of Jesus include:

- One Creator and the unity in diversity of human beings
- All humans are made in God's image
- The call of Abraham to be a blessing to all nations/fami-
  lies/cultures/clans
- Freeing enslaved people and rejecting God's talk to support
  enslavement
- Jesus' announcement of the Kindom of God
- Jesus' respect for people of diverse traditions

This tradition, begun in order to be a blessing to all in-groups, was distorted to support exclusive in-grouping, dehumanization, and violence:

- taking land by force
- hunting down and capturing people
- subjugating and enslaving anyone, not Christian

They did overwhelm the Moors or "Saracens" and began to kill and persecute Muslims, Jews, and other groups in a bloody period called the Spanish Inquisition. My Moorish ancestors became refugees and fled to southern Germany.

This was just the beginning of the violence authorized by what we now call the Doctrines of Discovery.

On This Continent

I asked Jay Bowen, an elder of the Upper Skagit Tribe, what a baby born among them could expect three hundred years ago. He responded:

- food
- shelter
- health care
- education
- freedom to follow your calling
- a voice in the governance of the tribe
- a wisdom tradition about how to be human together

To me, this sounds like the Kindom of God. It is estimated that up to 100 million people lived in what we call North America. Were not these people among the families, nations, tribes, clans, cultures, and religions to be blessed through Abraham's children?

Within two centuries, 95 percent of the population had died through disease, starvation, biological warfare, and murder.

Remember Your Identity

As you read these words, you may be having some strong feelings. It's not easy to write. Please take a moment and remember our baptismal identity. Our security is not in our confirmation bias. Our security is in our God-given belovedness. We are beloved as we are, wherever in the cycle of orientation, disorientation, and new orientation we are. Allowing ourselves to be challenged is an act of trust in God.

Dividing Spoils

Christopher Columbus came back from lands new to the Europeans with a political problem: How would Europeans divide these lands without entering into war with each other? The answer from Pope Alexander the V was that whoever first "discovered" a land could report it, claim the land, and claim the people as their property. The humanity of people was reduced to a game of "dibs." What happened to Muslims and Jews in the Iberian Peninsula would be replicated in these "discovered" lands. This purported divine sanction was used in Africa, Oceana, and on this continent. The race of "discovery" was on.

How would you feel if I "discovered" your house and claimed that I owned it? What if I did this by unintentionally or deliberately bringing disease to your relatives, destroying your food sources, murdering your people, forcing you out of your house, and enslaving you?

Thomas Jefferson cited the Papal documents and European countries' charters, which established the Doctrines of Discovery as international law. The Doctrines of Discovery continued to be cited as legal precedent in Supreme Court cases as recently as 2005.[32] We are only beginning to reckon with the impacts of colonization upon the human beings of Turtle Island.[33] European rulers used exclusive in-grouping and dehumanization with the blessing of the church to steal land, commit genocide, and enslave human beings.

When Christian groups arrived on the shores of this continent, they accepted and benefited from the exclusive in-grouping, dehumanization, and violence blessed by the Doctrines of Discovery. It is important for us all to recognize this and not fall into the trap of blaming Catholics in general for our shared history. These Doctrines were established before the Protestant movement and continued to be accepted as faithful. We all have a dog in this show. Protestants participated in colonization, too. These Doctrines function like a virus in our theology, songs, liturgies, and ethical teachings. Only recently have congregations started to stop singing Onward Christian Soldiers and other hymns that are similar.

The Doctrines of Discovery claimed to offer Divine sanction for colonization by European governments. It morphed into the more secular notion of manifest destiny. One can easily draw a straight line between the Doctrine of Discovery to Christian Nationalism, White Christian Supremacy, and hate groups that justify their deplorable ideologies.

The people best able to counter this ideology are, therefore, Christian churches and their members. Countering them does not mean trying to stop these groups from speaking. It means doing our work to repent of our exclusive in-grouping, dehumanization, and the violence we have either benefited from or engaged in. It means acting in partnership with other wisdom traditions in the healing and creation of the world. In other words, Christian communities are being once again invited to hear: The time is fulfilled, and the Kindom of God has come near; repent and believe in the good news.

Re-Membering Us

We have often torn ourselves apart as members of the human family. Christians have often used the Christian tradition in a way that supported, authorized, and excused exclusive in-grouping, dehumanization, and violence. Many Christians still do today, consciously or unconsciously.

We have become dis-membered from each other. I believe that God is re-membering us. God is bringing us back to each other. God is at work in the world, influencing us to remember ourselves as humans. We do not have to live in dehumanizing, murderous ways.

Many Christian organizations have repudiated the Doctrines of Discovery. On March 30, 2023, Pope Francis repudiated the Doctrines of Discovery. These are important steps, but only a step on the road to healing.

I encourage you to read the statements these churches have made.[34] Relationship, respect, and restitution are required next steps to facilitate healing for all of us and to build a better future together. We are better together.

Jesus' invitation to God's Way of Mutuality seemed unlikely in his time. How could the people oppressed by the Roman Empire recover from all the harm done to them and that they had done to one another? His message encourages us to change directions and trust that God is re-membering us to ourselves, one another, and God's beloved earth.

Jesus continues to invite us to change directions today and follow him into our common humanity.

Section Two Bible Studies

Jesus Honoring Our Common Humanity

Luke 15:1-6

Now all the tax-collectors and sinners were coming near to listen to him. And the Pharisees and the scribes were grumbling and saying, 'This fellow welcomes sinners and eats with them.' So he told them this parable: 'Which one of you, having a hundred sheep and losing one of them, does not leave the ninety-nine in the wilderness and go after the one that is lost until he finds it? When he has found it, he lays it on his shoulders and rejoices. And when he comes home, he calls together his friends and neighbors, saying to them, "Rejoice with me, for I have found my sheep that was lost."

Reflection

Tax collectors were lowly toll booth operators for the Romans. Those spoken of here were Jewish people who had no other economic opportunity to feed their families. They were seen as traitors. Sinners were not necessarily people with low ethics. Most often they were people who had no economic resources to do the rituals of their tradition.

Who you welcomed and with whom you ate was very important in 1st century Mediterranean culture. The status of your guests at the table with you became your status. People were expected to relate to people of a similar status or caste.

Jesus' story is simple yet layered with cultural meaning. Every shepherd was allowed a 15 percent loss rate on long trips to find food for the sheep. No shepherd would leave ninety-nine sheep to find one. Jesus says that, for God, there are no acceptable losses.

Jesus regularly and publicly engaged with people of low status, as well as with people of higher status. He created a community of people who had power with each other, not over each other. He created a community of people who strove to know and live according to the truth that only one status matters: Child of God. Jesus risked his life for his people because, for God, there are no acceptable losses.

Hey, What About This Verse?

Matthew 28:26-28

Go therefore and make disciples of all nations, baptizing them in the name of the Father and of the Son and of the Holy Spirit, and teaching them to obey everything that I have commanded you.

Reflection

This passage is often interpreted to mean that Jesus is saying Christians must convert all people to become Christians or else God's love is not accessible to them. The great commission of the church is to make everyone like us. This is part of a larger understanding of Christianity that says that Christianity is the only way to God and God's only way to us.

In this passage, Jesus expands his earlier command to the disciples about the geographic location of their mission. These twelve Jesus sent out with the following instructions: 'Go nowhere among the Gentiles and enter no town of the Samaritans' (Matthew 10:5). This was not a permanent limitation, but a community in which to begin to announce the Kindom of God.

In Matthew 28, Jesus expanded the geographical and cultural scope. Disciples are now working throughout the world and can include people of every *mishpachah*.

The Christian Scriptures were written in Greek, the most common written language in the Mediterranean world. Greek is different from English. The word we translate as "of" has a range of meanings, including "among." In this context of expanding the possible geography for the disciples, the translation "among" makes the most sense.[35] Let's read this verse with the word "among": Go therefore and make disciples among all nations, baptizing them in the name of the Father and of the Son and of the Holy Spirit.... This translation suggests that Jesus' community can include people of all cultures and traditions but does not require it for God to love and accept them.

"Among all nations" is about what land and cultural contexts Jesus' teachings can be taught, not saying that all people must join the church or be forever damned. It's about geography. It is not a claim that all must become Christian.

The traditional translation is not necessarily the best. As Christianity became a part of the Roman Empire and its descendants, the Christian faith was used to bless the colonization of other people's lands. The traditional translation offered divine approval for this, as empires required people to become Christian as a means of control and as an explanation for why what they were doing was right.

Even if we keep the translation of "make disciples of," we still must take the rest of the text seriously, including: "Teaching them to obey everything I have commanded you." What did Jesus teach? To love God and neighbor, that everyone is our neighbor, and that, for instance, the Samaritan's own tradition taught him to love God and neighbor enough to risk his life for a stranger. Jesus taught this out of faithfulness to his tradition's teachings of One Creator and the call of Abraham.

I recognize that many people have oriented their entire lives to trying to convert other people to Christianity because of their interpretation of this passage. For many years, I did, too. I still rejoice when someone becomes a part of Jesus' community. I also rejoice when people find lives of meaning and service in other traditions.

The traditional translation and interpretation of this passage suggests that Christianity is an exclusive in-group that has exclusive access to God and, therefore, is superior. This has led to the dehumanization of people of other traditions and cultures, which in turn led to motivating and justifying violence against them in the name of God. Dehumanization and violence are not faithful to what Jesus commanded his disciples to do. Jesus commanded his disciples to love their enemies. Christians sometimes reduce love to making other people like us or claiming our superiority over them. When it is, Christians neglect the weightier matters of the law and fail to love people as they are. Further, Christians begin to harass each other, judge each other, and begin to doubt and question God's love for each of us, wondering who is sufficiently Christian for God to accept.

It is not up to us to determine how the Creator may reach out to people in various cultural contexts and times. I am grateful that the

Creator reached out to me in the Christian faith. Still, it is beyond my "pay grade" to assume that the Creator can only reach other people through me and my tradition. I do not determine where the Holy Wind blows.

Section Three: Born into Empire

Key Question: How did the originating leader(s) of our tradition work for change to honor the unity and diversity of humanity?

Summary: Many of us recognize the divisions between us. We know these divisions undermine the peace of our communities. The question of this section is what our tradition teaches about working to honor everyone's human dignity. The Abrahamic tradition of One Creator blessing all the groups, cultures, and traditions of the world educated and shaped Jesus, preparing him for a response to the crisis of Roman occupation. He summarized his vision in the term "the Kindom of God." This Kindom is available to everyone, even the Romans who enforced the occupation. We remain vulnerable to the temptations of people in Jesus' day, but he continues to call us to honor the unity and diversity of human beings.

Chapter Eleven: Jesus' Life in Nazareth

Jesus grew up in Nazareth in Galilee. Nazareth was a very small town on a hillside overlooking the farmlands of the valley of Har Megiddo. Before the Romans came, many families in Nazareth had small farm plots on that fertile soil. Even in the best of years, these farms would produce barely enough to survive. Families would plant, grow, harvest, store, and process almost all the goods they needed to survive. They might trade some excess they had for other things they needed. They would also gather what they needed in the hills and lakes nearby. In a subsistence economy, life was hard but good.

In the year 63 BCE, the Roman Empire conquered the land, placed soldiers there, and began to extract money and goods for their own benefit. This is what they did to all their colonies.

The Romans installed a taxation system. Scholars such as Marcus Borg estimate that the overall taxation was between 38 to 43 percent. This was unsustainable in a subsistence economy. When crops were good, people could pay. When crops were not so good, they went into debt. The debt piled up. Then, one day, their land was taken and given to a wealthy Roman. This wealthy Roman would hire a manager for all their lands who would then hire people to work on land stolen by the Romans. No wonder Jesus told so many stories about managers and laborers!

By the time Jesus was thirteen, all the land in Galilee was owned by three wealthy Romans. Imagine how devastating that was to Jesus' family and neighbors and how powerless they felt. They were forced to stand in a marketplace and hope they got hired for the day for just enough money to last one day. This led to a society in which:

- 10 percent of people were homeless or had no resources
- 80 percent were poor

- 5 percent were middle-class
- 5 percent were wealthy[36]

The Romans benefited from all the stolen goods, stolen land, and the people's work. In Matthew 25, Jesus tells a story about this system. The landowner said, "I reap where I do not sow, and I gather where I do not scatter seed."[37] This landowner is not God, as we will cover in a later Bible study.

The Romans were a kingdom of greedy bullies. The Romans imposed what we could call a domination culture on people. They believed that might makes right.

Exile at Home

The Jewish tradition reminded Jesus and his community that their ancestors had lived through similar circumstances. In the 6th century, many were taken from the Jewish land of Judah to the land of Babylon. There, they sat by the rivers and wept. In that land, they wrote down their scriptures to keep them alive. While in Babylon, the prophet Isaiah spoke words of hope: One day, God would make a highway for the people to go back home. While that might not be soon, they could live in the truth of that promise today. This message kindled a hope beyond hope. Their freedom would be made possible by a Suffering Servant who would use nonviolent means to change the hearts of their captors. These enslaved Jewish people were later freed from exile in Babylon.

Biblical scholar N.T. Wright writes that, in Jesus' day, the Jewish people were experiencing an Exile at Home. They could taste Egypt and Babylon through the Roman occupation. It filled their senses during the day and haunted their dreams at night.

In a situation of such enforced scarcity, people sometimes turn against each other. Some grew angry and engaged in violence. Some blamed themselves and others, saying that if people were more faithful, God would change their situation. Some tried to escape to remote areas. Some said that when Rome comes to you, do as the Romans do. Some gave up any hope at all. We can see people with the same responses today.

Empires like Rome kept their thieving system intact by pitting people against each other. They turned people against each other even though they were all oppressed by the same system. Human beings have a natural in-group bias against other groups, but our chosen rivalries don't always make logical sense. Hitler turned the understandable anxiety of the German people after WWI against Jews, the Roma people, and LGBTQIA+ people. His own White Nationalist movement, of course, was the real threat. The same kind of thing happened in India when people of the Sikh tradition were made out to be a threat. We see the same kind of thing happening in the United States against our Jewish, Muslim, Indigenous, Black, Hispanic/Latinx, immigrant, and Asian American siblings. It is happening to the LGBTQIA+ community in Hungary, Russia, and the United States. It is happening to the Uighur population in China.

Powerful communicators can turn our in-group bias and anxiety into bias and bigotry against each other. They distract us from the unjust system through fear of each other to keep their rigged system intact.

Distracted

When we read the Christian Scriptures, we notice that people were split up into lots of groups in the 1st century. The word "distracted" comes from a Latin word that means to be "drawn apart." They created labels for

- People of different cultures and nations: Roman, Greek, Syrophoenician, Egyptian, Syrian, Israelite, and Samaritan
- Groups who all had a different response to the occupation of the Roman Empire: Chief Priests, Sadducees, Pharisees, Essenes, and Zealots
- People of different regions within Israel: Judean, Samaritan, and Galilean
- People in poverty trying to survive: Sinner, Tax Collector, Prostitute, and the Poor

That's a lot of in-groups and a lot of opportunity for exclusive in-grouping, dehumanizing each other, and escalating violence. It made a lot of people feel that they were surrounded by enemies and that help was far away. The Roman Empire intentionally distracted people from one another's common humanity.

Mary taught Jesus the Abrahamic tradition. She taught him about One Creator. She taught him that all humans are made in God's image. She taught him that God did not consent to blessing an unjust society and that God freed those enslaved. She taught that God sends truth-tellers to help us find a faithful path again. As he grew up, he saw all these in-groups. He saw the dehumanization. He saw people suffering under Roman-imposed scarcity. God called him to do something about it. Jesus responded to Roman occupation, exclusive in-grouping, and mutual dehumanization from the foundational values of the Abrahamic tradition:

- the Unity of the Creator and the Unity in Diversity of Humans
- recognizing other in-groups as human and working for the well-being of other in-groups
- countering dehumanization by speaking well of other in-groups

Let's consider a brief overview of how he lived these values in public. Jesus

- ate with sinners and tax collectors
- stayed overnight in a Samaritan village
- debated in public with a Syrophoenician woman
- stood up for a woman caught in adultery
- healed a Roman centurion's servant

You will likely be able to come up with more examples.

Working for Unity

Jesus engaged in public leadership to help his people counter the exclusive in-grouping and mutual dehumanization made worse by the Roman occupation. He realized that the Abrahamic tradition proposed a course of action, a strategy, for the times when we are divided when we feel like we are enemies of each other. He believed that people did not have to live by the Roman rules of exclusive in-grouping and bullying. He was willing to spend his time and risk his life to recognize the unity of the human family because that is what our God of love wants for us. Many people felt the power and possibility of this reminder of how to live.

The Romans saw that power, too. They knew that if people started seeing each other as human, their days of profiting from others would end. Jesus was no dummy. He knew how they would respond. So, he thought very carefully not only about the values and vision of the Abrahamic tradition but also how he would lead.

We are often distracted torn apart from one another. Some, in my view, distort Jesus' teachings to support this distraction. Jesus refused to be distracted from his fellow humans and called his disciples to follow him into our common humanity.

Chapter Twelve: Jesus' Way of Leadership

When I was in third grade, three students in my school began to beat people up when we played football. Yes, we played tackle football during recess! They would select a target and then hit them when we were in a pile so the teachers didn't see. As students, we couldn't go to recess if we didn't complete our work, so we just stopped doing it. Several classes of students were "having trouble" getting their work done until the teachers figured out what was happening.

We all are tempted to behave differently when bullies are around. Imagine if the bullies have a standing army. Imagine if the bullies could put you on a cross if you misbehaved. Imagine if they said the gods were on their side and there was no possibility for positive change.

Not Their First Rodeo

In Jesus' day, the Exile had come home in the form of the Roman Empire of bullies and thieves. The Jewish Tradition contained stories about similar times.

In the 6th century BCE, many Israelites were taken to the land of Babylon. Until then, they memorized their scriptures. In that land, they wrote down their scriptures to ensure they would not be lost. In that land, the first creation story in Genesis was inspired to counter another creation story. The Babylonian story proposed that the gods had created human beings to be slaves. This story claimed divine approval for exclusive in-grouping, dehumanization, and violence. The first creation story in the Hebrew Scriptures was intended to cast a different vision of who we are and how we can live together. The prophet Isaiah wrote of a leader called the Suffering Servant who would use nonviolent means to change their captor's hearts. However, they didn't need to wait for the reality of this vision to come later. They could live the vision during their enslavement in Babylon until they were free and healed. Jesus led in the same way in his day. He calls us to do the same in our own.

Isaiah also reminded them that such healing is the birthright of every human being and every in-group.

> It is too light a thing that you should be my servant
> to raise up the tribes of Jacob
> and to restore the survivors of Israel;
> I will give you as a light to the nations,
> that my salvation may reach to the end of the
> earth.
> Isaiah 49:6

The word "salvation" in scripture means healing, being brought to wholeness. It is a "salve" for our wounding ways. It encompasses not only individuals but groups, animals, plants, and the ecosystem. This healing is not just for one in-group but for all in-groups. Healing in its fullness is peace and justice realized for all.

A Deeper Look at Jesus' Baptism

To understand how Jesus responded to the kingdom of the bullies in his time, the Roman Empire, let's return to his baptism. When Jesus was baptized, he heard a voice from above saying, "You are my Son, the beloved; with you, I am well pleased."

The first part of this passage is a quote from Psalm 2, a poem and prayer used in coronations of a ruler of Israel. In that prayer, God calls the Hebrew ruler "my son." This is not just a claim to power but a call to responsibility. The king would be expected to live out the values of the God who called Abraham. The king would be one of the Children of God even while leading their siblings. Likewise, Jesus was not to be a bully oriented to the Roman way but to live by the core values of the Abrahamic tradition.

The second part of the passage refers to the leadership of the Suffering Servant in Isaiah. Jesus would not respond to the Roman occupation of his nation with despair, escape, blaming, violence, or going along with the kingdom of bullying. He would remember the dignity of all human beings and his own dignity, engaging in leadership without violence through which the whole society, including the Romans, would be transformed.

The Christian Scriptures portray Jesus as the anointed one who would restore the people to freedom through nonviolent means. He invited people to begin their work:

- accepting God's invitation to freedom from the ways of the Roman Empire
- recognizing their full humanity even within the Empire
- while remembering the humanity even of the Romans themselves

Jesus was a leader in the Abrahamic tradition. He was dedicated to the idea of One Creator. He was dedicated to the idea that he and his in-group were called to be a blessing to all the other in-groups. He was dedicated to the idea that all people are made in God's image. That meant that things needed to change and that the Romans were human, too. They also were trapped in the domination culture of their day. They caused suffering, but they were suffering, too.

Nowhere is this more powerfully stated than in the story about the centurion. In this passage, a centurion in Capernaum asks Jesus to heal his servant. When the centurion trusts that Jesus can mediate healing from a distance, Jesus makes it clear that God brings healing to people of every in-group and tradition.

> When Jesus heard him, he was amazed and said to those who followed him, "Truly I tell you, in no one in Israel have I found such faith. I tell you, many will come from east and west and will eat with Abraham and Isaac and Jacob in the kingdom of heaven, while the heirs of the kingdom will be thrown into the outer darkness, where there will be weeping and gnashing of teeth."
> Matthew 8:10-12

Throughout Christian history, this passage has been interpreted in an Antisemitic way. This is a misinterpretation. It's a critique of attitudes and behaviors, not a dehumanization of a group. Jesus, no doubt, understood that some among his Jewish community might say the Roman centurion's servant should not be healed because he was not part of their in-group. While his critique was originally directed to some among his own people, it is, more broadly, a critique of anyone who uses a wisdom tradition to claim to control access to God's love. Ironically, when we interpret the passage in an Antisemitic way, we become guilty of the very behavior of which the text warns. When we claim to be "the heirs," Jesus has a few words of warning for us.

Paul would later celebrate that Jesus' new community was open to people of every culture, economic situation, and gender:

> There is no longer Jew or Greek, there is no longer
> slave or free, there is no longer male and female; for
> all of you are one in Christ Jesus.
> Galatians 3:28

Jesus didn't want to win the game the Romans were playing. He wanted to change the game, creating a game in which everyone wins together.

Jesus' Stump Speech

In Mark chapter one, we see the basic outline of Jesus' message wherever he went. This would have been his bumper sticker, yard sign, and hashtag:

> Now after John was arrested, Jesus came to Galilee,
> proclaiming the good news of God, and saying, "The
> time is fulfilled, and the kingdom of God has come
> near; repent, and believe in the good news."
> Mark 1:14-15

This passage is short. But to people in his day, Jesus' words had a whole universe of meaning. The time of waiting was over. It was time to begin to live God's Way of Mutuality during the rule of the bullies. God's Way of Mutuality is one way to translate the term "kingdom of God." Other terms include the Beloved Community and the Kindom of God.

To understand Jesus' vision, it is important to recognize the kingdom that Jesus was seeking to replace: a bullying, might-makes-right, winner-takes-all, violence-saves, dog-eat-dog kingdom of exploitation, theft, and murder. The Romans didn't invent it, and it has been practiced by many empires before and since. We can see signs of this in the United States.

Like many domination cultures before, the Romans claimed divine blessing for what they did. Augustus Caesar claimed to be the son of the god Apollo, the Roman god of war. On the coin of Tiberius Caesar was the phrase, "son of the divine Augustus." It is one thing to be in a bullying culture. It is another to think that God created it that way.

We often imagine that if we lived in such a time, we could easily resist such a culture. But experiments like the Stanford Prison and Milgram's experiment tell us a different story. All human beings, including you and I, are deeply impacted by social pressure: what our in-group expects us to do. It isn't just that there are some "bad apples" but that the apple barrel of culture impacts the apples. We are deeply impacted by the society around us, by authorities, and by our in-groups in ways difficult to perceive.

In this culture oriented to domination, Jesus announced that God's Way of Mutuality had come near. The time to change had come, and Jesus invited them to trust that something new could happen. They didn't have to let the Romans set the tone for how they would see themselves, each other, and God. They could respect the image of God in themselves, in people of diverse wisdom traditions, and even in the Romans. They, too, were caught up in a system of domination, and some longed to escape. Jesus taught his in-group to reorient to God's Way of Mutuality and begin the work of being the change they wished to see in the world.

This requires deep reflection, painful change, and renewed trust. But oh, what a relief it is when the shackles of a false life hit the ground, and we begin to truly honor the image of God in ourselves and each other.

We live today in a world of bullies and bullying. Sometimes, we participate in the bullying, and other times, we are bullied ourselves. Just as Jesus invited the disciples in his day, he invites us. Jesus continues to lead his disciples to see that a new way to live is near; God's Way of Mutuality is here. God invites us to change our ways and trust that we can be a part of something beautiful. We are free to move from an orientation to the way of bullying, become disoriented, and find a new orientation centered on God's dreams for the world.

Currently, we see this bullying in language by public leaders about members of the LGBTQIA+ community. A family member of mine recently told me that my support for that community was silly. He said, "Why do you feel it necessary to stand up for such a small group of people?" I responded, "Because they are people. First, it's transgender people, and then it's another group, and then it's all of us."

The path toward God's dream was not easy for Jesus. It is not easy for us. It is full of temptation and opportunities, challenges and blessings. Let's turn to those next.

Chapter Thirteen: Our Common Temptations

The path of resisting exclusive in-grouping and dehumanization of other groups is narrow. There are many temptations along the way. Jesus' temptations offer us a view into what to look out for.

Soon after his baptism, Jesus was sent into the wilderness to be tempted.

> Then Jesus was led up by the Spirit into the wilderness to be tempted by the devil. He fasted forty days and forty nights, and afterwards he was famished. The tempter came and said to him, "If you are the Son of God, command these stones to become loaves of bread." But he answered, "It is written, 'One does not live by bread alone, but by every word that comes from the mouth of God.'" Then the devil took him to the holy city and placed him on the pinnacle of the temple, saying to him, "If you are the Son of God, throw yourself down; for it is written, 'He will command his angels concerning you,' and 'On their hands they will bear you up, so that you will not dash your foot against a stone.'" Jesus said to him, "Again it is written, 'Do not put the Lord your God to the test.'" Again, the devil took him to a very high mountain and showed him all the kingdoms of the world and their splendor; and he said to him, "All these I will give you, if you will fall down and worship me." Jesus said to him, "Away with you, Satan! For it is written, 'Worship the Lord your God, and serve only him.'" Then the devil left him, and suddenly angels came and waited on him.
> Matthew 4:1-11

Jesus was baptized and then given a job: to announce God's Way of Mutuality. At this point in the story, Jesus should get an agent a media consultant, and be taken to Jerusalem on a stretch camel. There, he could have taken selfies with the powerful and famous. Instead, the Spirit led him into the wilderness for forty days of fasting.

The biblical storytellers often used numbers to help us see connections between stories. It rained for 40 days in the story about Noah and God's sadness over the violence on the earth. Moses went to the mountain for 40 days, and neither ate nor drank. The people of Israel spent 40 years in the desert–learning how to live differently from the domination culture that had taken over Egypt. The Gospel writers emphasize that Jesus' story is intertwined with these stories.

In this story, we see not only the temptations that Jesus faced but how domination culture tempts all of us. The devil here is not some dude in a red jumpsuit. He represents the unseen forces of a domination culture that tempt us to conform to its values and to its vision for a divided humanity. The term "devil" means "the deceiver." How often does a domination culture try to deceive us into believing we are not beloved or that we are the only ones who are beloved?

Short Term Needs

Jesus was tempted to place his own short-term, individual needs first. Jesus answered with a quote from Deuteronomy:

> He humbled you by letting you hunger, then by
> feeding you with manna, with which neither you
> nor your ancestors were acquainted, in order to
> make you understand that one does not live by
> bread alone, but by every word that comes from the
> mouth of the LORD.
> Deuteronomy 8:3

How often does our larger culture tempt us to place our short-term needs before our long-term needs? How often does our culture tempt us to put individual needs before our collective and environmental needs? How often does our culture tell us that our meaning is found in what we own?

Instead, Jesus trusted that his body's needs would be met in this wilderness as they had in the days of Moses and Miriam.

Status Keeping

Then Jesus was taken to the top of the Temple in Jerusalem and told to prove his identity by jumping off. This is the temptation of high status. Jesus was tempted to act out of his high status of being the Messiah.

How often does our culture tempt us to act out of privilege and status? How often do people of privilege thank God for their status while leaving the obvious second question unanswered: if God blessed you with high status and wealth, then did God curse others with poverty or low status?

At the 2014 Oscars, one actor thanked God for putting him in the position to win an Oscar. No doubt, it is a good thing that he thanked God for his life. But to thank God for such a blessing without noting the billions that live in poverty is something else. The actor who won Best Supporting Actress in Twelve Years a Slave responded differently. She stated her awareness that so much good has come to her from playing a role portraying a person whose life held so much pain. This is quite a difference!

Jesus refused to use his status to test God. He trusted God to care for him in God's own time. He did not need to prove it to himself or the tempter because he was secure in his baptismal identity. Further, he recognized the Abrahamic tradition of modesty and respect for God–and our equal status as human beings before God. Remember that as the "Son of Man," Jesus' job was not to rule over people but to rule together with people.

To rebuff the deceiver, he once again quoted scripture:

> Do not put the LORD your God to the test.
> Deuteronomy 6:16

The Big Cheese

Then, he was taken to a high mountain. In Biblical texts, mountains are often a symbol of political power. In this case, they were probably referring to Jesus being taken to Rome. Why the poetry instead of just naming it? Matthew was a Jewish Christian writing around the year 80. He could be asked to produce his writing by the police at any time–if he was not careful in what he wrote, he could have been arrested, his writing destroyed, and his community endangered. So, he used the poetic symbols of his people to stay free and convey his message.

On the high mountain of Rome, Jesus was offered Caesar's throne if he would worship his tempter.

How often are we tempted to use power over others to accomplish our well-intentioned goals? How often are we tempted to see violence as a saving power?

Jesus was unwilling to bow to the devil, the agent of the domination culture. He would only bow to God. He again quoted Deuteronomy:

> The LORD your God you shall fear; him you shall
> serve, and by his name alone you shall swear.
> Deuteronomy 6:13

Our Temptations

By writing this story, Matthew and the other gospel writers were not just trying to show us how Jesus is worthy to lead us because he resisted temptation. Matthew is trying to show us the ways that a domination culture tempts us: How a bullying culture, a culture of power over others can tempt us to

- act in fear for our own individual, short-term needs, exploiting other humans and the created world
- seek status over each other
- look for the quick fix through power over others

In this story, Jesus is an example of how to resist these temptations.

But where do we begin? We read scripture and study in our community, but we also relate and listen to ourselves and others. Below is a conversation between the Reverend Kelle Brown, pastor of Plymouth Church, United Church of Christ, Dr. Catherine Punsalan-Manlimos of Seattle University, and me. Together, we addressed how to resist the temptations of our own domination culture in the United States on our TV show, *Challenge 2.0*:

> Dr. Catherine Punsalan-Manlimos: I find myself seeing faces of some of my students and some of the students I've worked with. And it [my suggestion] would be: sit down with a young woman of color and listen to her story and listen to the harm she's experienced and how the experience of white supremacy and racism has

had a profound impact on her own sense of self-worth and the hard work she has to do to overcome that.

Rev. Dr. Kelle Brown: I think my invitation would be something like the one Peggy McIntosh heard, where she tried to deal with the oppression of her own life as a woman, and then it bridged her into the oppression of African American folk and other people of color. My invitation wouldn't be to read and to educate. My invitation would be to, say, find and own place where you don't feel you've been heard or listened to that is most broken, most vulnerable, where you need God, or whatever you believe in, to impact your life, and imagine that that can transform into empathy for the other. There's something about selfishness, but there's also something about the lack of self-care that we promote from the church that does not allow for folks to hear the other. And, so, I would say, start with you, though I believe in community and collectivity. I know in this individualistic society, start with yourself and find that place where God may allow a bridge to be born to the other.

Rev. Terry Kyllo: You know, I was bullied as a kid, in part because my Mother had multiple sclerosis. And so, people were afraid it was catching. And so folks distanced themselves from our family. And so, I agree with Kelle, with both of you, that we need to start with our own sense of pain and what was that like for me. And then, beyond that, then, learn about people of color from people of color. Quit learning about them from third parties on TV or on the internet that want to tell you about them and want to frame the debate. And when we go out and encounter, when I go and encounter my Muslim neighbors, when I go out and encounter someone, it's not just their humanity I'm finding. It's actually my own. Because we are all children of one God and we're all in this together. And our humanities are bound up with each other.

Matthew shows us how we can be tempted to use our status and privilege to maintain our dominance over others instead of striving for mutuality. Matthew is teaching us that to achieve our goals by violence and power over others is not God's way. The ends do not justify the means! Jesus shows disciples another way, trusting we are secure in our baptismal identity.

Yet, there is much work to do, and work takes power. How we understand power helps shape the way we work. Let's turn to that next.

Chapter Fourteen: Jesus' Vision of the Kindom of God

Jesus had a vision that was bigger than starting a chain of churches. He saw how his own people were being led away from the deep roots of his tradition. The domination culture of the Roman Empire, like many before and after, was dividing people from one another. Let's explore Jesus' vision and how it might apply to today.

Countering the Domination Distortion Field

In the 1950s, researcher Muzafer Sherif wanted to find out the minimal amount of difference between two groups that would create rivalry. He took two groups of boys from nearly identical backgrounds and formed two groups naming themselves the Eagles and the Rattlers at the Robbers Cave Camp. In the first week, they created a group. In the second week, they became aware of the other group. By the third, the two groups were vandalizing each other's camps, accusing the other group of terrible conspiracies, and creating dehumanizing language about each other.

> The boys at Robbers Cave needed nothing but isolation and competition to consider the other team almost instantaneously to be 'dirty bums,' to hold negative stereotypes about them, to avoid social contact with them, and to overestimate their own group's abilities.[38]
> Liliana Mason

The minimal amount of in-grouping necessary to create this was simply to have two groups.

This, and so much other research through the years, has shown us that exclusive in-grouping and dehumanization are not just a challenge of this moment but a central, ongoing challenge for our species. Our capacity to bond with a group is a beautiful thing. But we can identify so much with our group that we begin to dehumanize and, under the right circumstances, engage in violence toward other groups.

The minimal amount of in-grouping necessary to create this was **simply to have two groups.**

This, and so much other research through the years, has shown us that exclusive in-grouping and dehumanization are not just a challenge of this moment but a central, ongoing challenge for our species. Our capacity to bond with a group is a beautiful thing. But we can identify so much with our group that we begin to dehumanize, and, under the right circumstances, engage in violence toward other groups.

Dividing Wisdom

The Kingdom of Rome believed that the gods approved of their colonizing land, resources, and people. They understood human nature very well. Their leaders took advantage of common vulnerabilities to create and maintain their empire. They leveraged common vulnerabilities to preserve their power by

- dividing people into exclusive in-groups
- encouraging people to dehumanize each other
- creating a society in which people compete for status and power
- cultivating greed and fear so that people would collaborate with them
- imposing scarcity for basic needs
- deforming people's own wisdom tradition to confuse and disempower them
- encouraging despair

People were being overwhelmed by the Empire of Rome. Their very humanity was being eaten away by Rome's acidic domination culture. Early Christian writers used words like "flesh" or "the world" to refer to the culture of Rome that was corrupting their humanity. Remember, they had to speak in such poetic terms to avoid Roman persecution. The "flesh" of the domination culture brought such pain to people that they resorted to addictive and destructive behaviors.[39]

> Live by the Spirit, I say, and do not gratify the
> desires of the flesh. For what the flesh desires is
> opposed to the Spirit, and what the Spirit desires is
> opposed to the flesh; for these are opposed to each
> other, to prevent you from doing what you want.
> But if you are led by the Spirit, you are not subject
> to the law. Now the works of the flesh are obvious:
> fornication, impurity, licentiousness, idolatry,
> sorcery, enmities, strife, jealousy, anger, quarrels,
> dissensions, factions, envy, drunkenness, carousing,
> and things like these.
> Galatians 5:16-21

Jesus saw what the Roman domination culture was doing to people and, instead, offered them unity.

> Then Jesus went about all the cities and villages,
> teaching in their synagogues, and proclaiming the
> good news of the kingdom, and curing every disease
> and every sickness. When he saw the crowds, he had
> compassion for them, because they were harassed
> and helpless, like sheep without a shepherd.
> Matthew 19:35-36

Uniting Wisdom

Abraham's call was to create an in-group whose core value was to recognize others as human, to speak well of others, and, in humility, to offer their best to help others survive and thrive. Born under Roman occupation, **Jesus led from within the Abrahamic tradition.** He recognized people of all in-groups as human. He invited all people to participate in the Kindom of God amid the Kingdom of Rome. His hearers would have heard this in his stump speech: The Kindom of God has come near–let's change our ways and trust that we can participate in a new way to be human together. Every scripture Jesus references, everything he said, every act of healing, expresses his vision of the Kindom of God. Here is one:

> He unrolled the scroll and found the place where it
> was written:
> "The Spirit of the Lord is upon me,
> because he has anointed me
> to bring good news to the poor.
> He has sent me to proclaim release to the captives

and recovery of sight to the blind,
to let the oppressed go free,
to proclaim the year of the Lord's favor."
Luke 4:16-19

Isaiah wrote to those Jewish people enslaved in Babylon. The Suffering Servant referenced in this text was given a calling to change economic inequity, to free from jail leaders who refused to stay silent, to give people a vision of how we can live together, to free those oppressed in slavery, and to announce Jubilee: the cancellation of debts and return of land to their previous owners so all would have enough.

Jesus' first hearers would have understood that God's promise to those in Babylon was now being re-promised to those in the Kingdom of Rome. God's Way of Mutuality is God's love, grace, and peace in everyday life, in every aspect of human relationship: public, private, economic, political, personal, communal, body, mind, and environment.

In this Kindom, we recognize each other as human and work for a society in which everyone has:

- meaning
- relationships
- food
- shelter
- clothing
- medical care
- education
- a way to contribute to the community and the earth

Jesus knew that people were being distorted by the domination culture of the Roman Empire. He also knew that people tend to go with the flow, even in unjust systems. Throughout history and in many experiments, human beings too often go along with the crowd and follow orders to fit in—even when it is against their own well-being.

Jesus was called to be a leader in the Abrahamic tradition, to lead a community of those willing to risk behaving differently. He called people to this vision. He called people to join him in leadership to transform the Roman empire from within. Jesus wanted a conversion. Maybe not from one religion to another, but from a culture of domination to a culture of mutuality. He wanted a conversion of our hearts toward each other and God to

- the unity and diversity of human beings
- recognizing all in-groups as human, offering one another our best in humility
- resisting claims of divine affirmation for unjust systems
- power with each other instead of power over each other
- hope for our common future
- relationships of respect among God's diverse human beings
- stewardship of the earth and our fellow creatures

THIS is the vision. Not of beautiful churches—although buildings can be both beautiful and useful. Not of isolated Christian in-groups competing for Sunday morning statistics. A vision of following the way of God that is available to all humans who share in God's image. In Christianity, our baptismal identity includes the daily work of just such a conversion.

Among You

> Once Jesus was asked by the Pharisees when the kingdom of God was coming, and he answered, 'The kingdom of God is not coming with things that can be observed; nor will they say, "Look, here it is!" or "There it is!" For, in fact, the kingdom of God is among all y-all.'
> Luke 17:20-21

This Kindom would be embodied by a community of people gathered around the Abrahamic vision. It would be among all of us. This doesn't mean it belongs to us. The Kindom of God is, well, God's. It belongs to God, but God calls all of God's children together in it and shares it with us.

Yet, disciples of Jesus have continued here and there to strive for God's Kindom, for Jesus' vision, and to live out Abraham's call. Since Constantine's conversion of Christianity to serve the Roman Empire, our vision of the Kindom of God has itself been distorted. It has been reduced to either heaven when we die, to the church itself, or, worse, to church-blessed authoritarianism. We have often claimed to own the Kindom of God as if it is a McChristians franchise—another way to divide us from one another. Yet, disciples of Jesus have continued, at times, to strive for God's Kindom, for Jesus' vision, for Abraham's call.

The Church

Martin Luther was a Catholic monk, theologian, and Biblical scholar in the 1500s in Germany. He lived in a time when the word "church" was reduced to mean the institution of the church. Through much study, prayer, and sleepless nights, Luther realized the church was not fully faithful to Jesus's Kindom. He went on to redefine the church as "the community gathered around Word and Sacrament." He saw the church as the community of Christians, including those who were in leadership among them. Institutions may be necessary to support the ongoing work of the community through generations.

Many in the church named for him have reduced Luther's teaching. They imply that as long as people gather and engage in Word and Sacrament, they fulfill Jesus' vision. As in Luther's time, a reframing is helpful for us to be more faithful to that vision:

The church is the community formed in Word and Sacrament that is daily reoriented to, participates in and invites others toward the Kindom of God.

Jesus' community engages in both reflection and spiritual practices. These are great! But they are meant to form us for daily reorientation and participation in the Kindom of God. As Luther reminded us, this Kindom is coming of its own accord. The healing of the creation and the *mishpachah* of the world is the promise of the Creator. We are those who, along with many others, are invited to contribute to that healing in the here and now.

The Creator's Freedom

The Creator exercised God's freedom to call Abraham, Moses, and Jesus. **The Creator has the freedom to call others in their own language, culture, and context**. God values people of all families, nations, cultures, and religions. God blesses them. God has called people of all *mishpachah* to recognize one another as human and to love their neighbor as themselves. The Creator's vision is the birthright of every human.

> When Gentiles, who do not possess the law, do instinctively what the law requires, these, though not having the law, are a law to themselves. They show that what the law requires is written on their hearts, to which their own conscience also bears

witness.

Romans 2:14-15

This adds something to the definition of the church above: **The church is the community formed in Word and Sacrament that is daily reoriented to, participates in, invites others toward the Kindom of God,** *and partners with all wisdom communities in the healing and creation of the world.*

This is a pivotal point. Just as we honor the unity of the creation in monotheism, so we must also honor our unity in the God-given desire to heal our divisions, heal the creation, and build a better future. Without this kind of imagination, our very desire for the healing and creation of the world falls short by claiming only Christians can contribute to this healing. This is a subtle and powerful form of exclusive in-grouping.

In the midst of all else he said, Luther recognized that the Kindom of God is not the wholly owned subsidiary of Christians. This is why it's important in my description of the church that Christians can invite people "toward" the Kindom of God and not "into" it. In the Small Catechism he wrote of the meaning of the petition "Thy Kingdom come" in the Lord's Prayer:

> The kingdom of God comes indeed without our
> prayer, of itself; but we pray in this petition that it
> may come unto us also.
> Martin Luther, Small Catechism

We don't own the Kindom of God. We pray for it to come in its fullness. We pray that we might take our part in it. It is only in our arrogance and exclusive in-grouping that we assume that the only agents of the Kindom are among Christians.

Christians are equally vulnerable to exclusive in-grouping and dehumanization as any other group. This vulnerability is inherent to human beings, as the research at Robbers Cave Camp reveals. God's power frees us daily to see a future built with people of other wisdom traditions. Jesus believed that we don't have to live this way. At our best, Christians form a community committed to recognizing the humanity of other communities, eating together, sharing stories, working for the common good, and standing in public together. In doing so, we are faithful to the vision and character of the Creator, revealed to us through Jesus Christ. In such partnerships, we begin the very work of addressing the challenges we face today.

Section Three Bible Studies

Jesus Honoring Our Common Humanity

Matthew 25:14-30

'For it is as if a man, going on a journey, summoned his slaves and entrusted his property to them; to one he gave five talents, to another two, to another one, to each according to his ability. Then he went away. The one who had received the five talents went off at once and traded with them, and made five more talents. In the same way, the one who had the two talents made two more talents. But the one who had received the one talent went off and dug a hole in the ground and hid his master's money. After a long time the master of those slaves came and settled accounts with them. Then the one who had received the five talents came forward, bringing five more talents, saying, "Master, you handed over to me five talents; see, I have made five more talents." His master said to him, "Well done, good and trustworthy slave; you have been trustworthy in a few things, I will put you in charge of many things; enter into the joy of your master." And the one with the two talents also came forward, saying, "Master, you handed over to me two talents; see, I have made two more talents." His master said to him, "Well done, good and trustworthy slave; you have been trustworthy in a few things, I will put you in charge of many things; enter into the joy of your master." Then the one who had received the one talent also came forward, saying, "Master, I knew that you were a harsh man, reaping where you did not sow, and gathering where you did not scatter seed; so I was afraid, and I went and hid your talent in the ground. Here you have what is yours." But his master replied, "You wicked and lazy slave! You knew, did you, that I reap where I did not sow, and gather where I did not scatter? Then you ought to have invested my money with the bankers, and on my return I would have received what was my own with interest. So take the talent from him, and give it to the one with the ten talents. For to all those who have, more will be given, and they will have an abundance; but from those who have nothing, even what they have will be taken away. As for this worthless slave, throw him into the outer darkness, where there will be weeping and gnashing of teeth."

Reflection

The man in this passage is not God. The Jewish tradition taught that God had prohibited interest. What does God need of interest? The man in this passage accepts that he is a thief. Is God a thief? The Hebrew tradition teaches that "The Earth is the Lord's and the fullness thereof." Does God exploit the labor of others? The Hebrew tradition teaches sabbath and jubilee, not exploitation.

It is more likely that the "man on a journey" is a reference to Caesar.

Burying money in the ground was considered a way to safely hide money–and since God controlled what came from the ground, it was not your fault if something happened.

Most people in Jesus' day and area considered trading to be theft. They thought the economic pie was only so big. They would have seen these managers as thieves. The third manager in the story tells the truth about the Roman Empire: It was a domination system that stole from people. In this passage, Jesus shares his central critique of the domination culture of Rome. In the Empire, the focus was money and power. In the following story in Matthew, he shares his vision of the Kindom of God, where what matters is people and our care for people who are vulnerable.

Hey, What About This Verse?

John 14:6

Jesus said to him, "I am the way, and the truth, and the life. No one comes to the Father except through me."

Reflection

This passage is often quoted to indicate Jesus' intention that Christians be an exclusive in-group, and that God authorizes this.

The first indication that this might not be the best interpretation of this verse is that the I AM in this passage evokes the I AM in Exodus. This name for God implies that the Creator is beyond any definition we might make and beyond our control or ownership. It is odd to take a passage that refers to the mystery of God and use it to claim that we know the only way to this mystery and, therefore, are superior to other traditions.

Second, scholars Brockman and Habito remind us that "through me" refers to Jesus as the "logos" or divine wisdom become human. It does not necessarily mean "through belief in Jesus' divinity" but rather that the divine wisdom through whom the world was created is available to everyone by the action of Jesus–not our action.[40] John 1:9-13 reminds us that this logos is already in people around the world because all have been created through it. The claim of the passage all together is that Jesus embodies and reveals the character of God and, thus, the true character of human beings.

People often quote this passage without any consideration of the way that Jesus walked and taught.

When asked about this verse, I often respond, "I believe that Jesus is the way, the truth, and the life. So, we then need to consider the way that Jesus lived and embodied the way, the truth, and the life in the world." Jesus:

- loved God
- risked his life to free his neighbors from the coercive fear of Roman terror through the cross
- recognized people of diverse traditions and cultures as humans and children of the same Creator
- engaged in table fellowship, offered healing, and publicly debated with people of various traditions, economic classes, and statuses

Additionally, Philippians 2 tells us that the "mind of Christ" is one of service to and equality with others, not seeking to dominate or compete for status with each other. Honoring the humanity of all people respecting people of diverse traditions, classes, and statuses is the "way to God" and the way that God has given all people. As Christians, we are invited into this way through Jesus Christ. This way is the way to life.

Section Four: Three Great Teachings

Key Question: What is our tradition's basic understanding of love and the ethical framework for living out love?

Summary: Traditions teach us how to live in the real world in real time—and so it is vital that we continually explore the core of our tradition. A challenge for Christians is that within 70 years, we lost touch with the Hebrew tradition—the tradition of Jesus. In this section, we cover the Three Great Teachings, the meaning of "love" in the Christian Scriptures, and the meaning of sacrifice. The meaning of sacrifice in the Hebrew tradition was tragically lost, creating misunderstandings of the meaning of the life, death, and resurrection of Jesus. These misunderstandings have led many Christians to see people of other traditions as outside of God's love.

Chapter Fifteen: Let There Be

And God saw everything that God had made, and
indeed, it was very good. And there was evening
and there was morning, the sixth day.
Genesis 1:31

We are alive. We can sense the world. We have our inner conversations and are aware of our existence, the existence of others, the earth, and the cosmos. Hopefully, we have the courage and space to feel awe at this. We tremble at the fact of our existence. We are grateful for our existence, and all that walk the path of life with us.

Monotheism teaches that one Divine Presence is the source of all that is. The Abrahamic tradition, one among many monotheistic traditions, teaches that this Divine Presence created the universe with only a word. To be in awe of the Creator and to be in awe of the creation are part of a holy circle, leading one to the other.

The whole of wisdom is awe of the Lord,
and in all wisdom there is the fulfillment of the
teachings.
Ecclesiasticus 19:20

The Abrahamic tradition teaches that God values creation. God sees that it is "good, very good." **This is the beginning of ethics and the core of morality.** Everything and everyone we interact with is good in and of themselves and thus of intrinsic worth. When human beings interact with creation, the value of each part of creation and each person must be held together. We may compete for resources, but we compete as equally valuable beings in a limited universe. The practice of ethics is to discern how to behave as part of a good and valuable creation. The purpose of our teachings is to help us embody, in the real world and in real time, the value of each part of the creation, including ourselves.

We Don't Own God

In 2016, after much discernment with my bishops, pastors, deacons, and family, I left parish ministry to counter anti-Muslim bigotry. Since then, I have engaged with over a hundred congregations to prepare them for relationships with people of all wisdom traditions.

In these engagements, I would always teach about monotheism and the core teaching of the Abrahamic tradition to "Love the Lord your God with all your heart, soul, strength, and mind and your neighbor as you love yourself." As the conversation went forward, I noticed that many folks reduced "love God" into

- loving our idea of God as if it is God
- loving "our God" versus "their god"

How could the idea of One Creator and Blesser of all the families of the earth be reduced into us versus them? Human beings are vulnerable to exclusive in-grouping. Traditions that emerge to resist exclusive in-grouping, traditions inspired by a pluralistic vision, can get twisted to do the opposite, saying: "You are human if you believe like us…." This is a constant temptation.

The Abrahamic teachings of the value of all people and cultures have been obscured with:

- 1900 years of being detached from Jesus' culture, context, and Hebrew teachings
- 1400 years of being the cheerleader for domination culture
- 500 years of Doctrines of Discovery

But we can still turn around. We can begin to see, to live.

After many walks in the forest with my dog Ginger and conversations with leaders of many traditions, I realized Christians need a clarification of the Abrahamic tradition. Here is the first core teaching of our tradition:

Love God more than our in-group and tradition.

This can be expressed in less traditional terms. This is how I would express it to atheists, agnostics, and to those of non-theistic traditions:

Love all of life more than our in-group and tradition.

This expression can help those of us committed to following Jesus in the Abrahamic tradition. Loving God with our whole self means loving God more than our in-group, more than our tradition, more than anything. But all too often, we humans replace love of the Creator with claims of superiority of our in-groups, our beliefs, and our prayers. The first commandment was always intended to guard us against such superiority with awe of the Creator. In Jesus' prayer, the words "Our Father" mean the God of all creation and all humans. We are praying on behalf of all the creation. God is not our property, nor is God only the God of our in-group. To love God is to love all the Creator has made. To love God is to value all that the Creator values. Everything and everyone.

A Second Is Like It

> "Teacher, which commandment in the law is the greatest?" He said to him, "'You shall love the Lord your God with all your heart, and with all your soul, and with all your mind." This is the greatest and first commandment. And a second is like it: 'You shall love your neighbor as yourself.' On these two commandments hang all the law and the prophets.
> Matthew 22:36-40

God created a diverse creation, and God values each part, each person, each tribe, and each tradition. In conversation with a fellow Hebrew teacher, Jesus teaches us to love our neighbor as we love ourselves. This teaching arises from the insight of the unity in diversity of all creation in the first commandment. Jesus repeated the common view that the teachings in the Torah and all truth-telling of the prophets arise from these two core teachings.

This teaching reminds us that our well-being is directly connected to the well-being of others. If I take all the firewood I will be warm and afraid. My neighbors will be cold and angry. Peace, safety, and our well-being are simply not possible unless all our neighbors have enough. Some see this teaching as starry-eyed and unrealistic. It actually forms the basis of our own well-being. It teaches us the clear-sighted and pragmatic reality that only when all have access to the basic needs of life, our daily bread, can our well-being be possible.

In my work with Christian congregations, I have noticed that we tend to reduce the word "love" to warm feelings, moral outrage expressed on social media, and yelling at the TV.

The word "love" here and in most Christian Scriptures is the

Greek word *agape*: self-risking love. Love is risking ourselves to increase the well-being of ourselves, our neighbors, society, and the creation we are a part of.

Even this definition can be troublesome when we decide that we know what well-being looks like for our neighbor without talking to our neighbor. The Doctrines of Discovery taught Western Christians that we can reduce people's well-being to becoming Christians so they can go to heaven when they die. They justified cultural genocide, enslavement, and actual genocide with a get-into-heaven-free card while enslaving people in the here and now. This continues to impact our perspectives, actions, and policies today.

We also tend to reduce the call of this core teaching by limiting who we consider our "neighbor." Many white Christian supremacists believe that people, unlike them, are not really their neighbors, even not fully human. But, in his teachings and life, Jesus is clear that the word neighbor applies to every human being and every human community.

Loving our neighbors as we love ourselves means discerning **with our neighbors** how we can work for our mutual well-being, honoring one another's needs. This is hard work and often imperfect, but it is the holy and good work of building our future together.

This second of the Three Great Teachings directly applies to dehumanization. Dehumanization is powered by a perceived threat by another in-group to what we love. Our love for our own in-group can be weaponized against us in such a way that we believe another in-group deserves to be exempted from love. Love requires we monitor, question, and manage our own moral outrage. Love requires that we inspect our fears and feelings. It requires us not to reduce our love to our own in-group.

The first teaching guides us to honor the Creator above all things, even our tribe and tradition. This teaching reminds us that being human includes loving all in-groups. While we love our in-group and even protect it from harm, we are not freed from the love of other in-groups—even those with whom who we are at odds. This teaching guides us to see others as human. This teaching guides us to remember that humans and all of life are bound together and cannot be separated without great harm to all. This teaching guides us to refrain from allowing our love for our in-group to become exclusive.

A Third is Like Them

The second core teaching is embedded in the first. But as I gave presentations in churches and civic groups, I realized something was missing. I began to realize that a third great teaching is embedded in the first two:

Steward a thriving ecosystem and an equitable economy.

To honor the Creator who blesses all people and the earth includes managing our needs, and our consumption, with the needs of all life and the future of all life on this planet: to love all of life more than our in-group and tradition.

> God blessed them, and God said to them, 'Be fruitful
> and multiply, and fill the earth and subdue it; and
> rule the fish of the sea and over the birds of the air
> and over every living thing that moves upon the
> earth.'
> Genesis 1:28

The Creator has given human beings the responsibility to steward the earth and every living thing. While the earth meets our needs, our needs are not the only consideration. Each part of the creation is valuable in and of itself.

The stewarding of the ecosystem must be held in tension with how human beings live what we produce and consume. In contrast, Western culture has often valued ever-increasing production and consumption as the ultimate good, the very sign of civilization.

Jay Julius, a leader of the Lummi Nation, shared:

> Jay Julius: The storyteller says the Creator created heaven
> and earth, then created water, then created the whales
> and fish. I think what's important in all traditional sto-
> ries from Lummi [Nation], from Europe, from Alaska,
> from Hawaii: Humans weren't first. I think ancient
> storytellers talked about common sense, caretaking,
> stewardship, ways to take care of this gift, this garden.

What we produce and consume, and its impact on the ecosystem is held in tension with the just distribution of these resources.

> Hear this, you that trample on the needy,
> and bring to ruin the poor of the land,

saying, "When will the new moon be over
so that we may sell grain;
and the sabbath,
so that we may offer wheat for sale?
We will make the ephah small and the shekel great,
and practice deceit with false balances,
buying the poor for silver
and the needy for a pair of sandals,
and selling the sweepings of the wheat."
Amos 8:4-6

In this passage, Amos speaks about the actions of individuals, economic practices, and the use of religion to create an unjust economic system. In Amos, God later declares the consequences of that unfair system. The whole Abrahamic tradition includes teaching about equitable distribution to meet basic human needs. While there is no one economic theory proposed in the Abrahamic tradition, every financial system is measured by how equitable it is for all people.

It is not righteousness that you turn your faces
towards East or West. But the righteousness is to
believe in Allah and the Last Day, and the Angels,
and the Book, and the Prophets, and to give of your
wealth out of love for Him, to your kin and orphans
and the needy and the wayfarer and those who ask,
and for the ransom of slaves.
Quran 2:177

Hebrew tradition teaches the same:

Whoever oppresses the poor shows contempt for
their Maker, but whoever is kind to the needy
honors God.
Proverbs 14:31

The religion of *homo economicus* has led us to vast economic inequality, environmental collapse, and collective despair. The ecological and economic crises we are facing are, at root, a crisis of meaning. Many see what they produce and consume as the meaning of their lives. They are willing to sacrifice themselves, their families, and the future of the earth to attain this sense of meaning. The Three Great Teachings offer a deeper vision of who we are as humans who are a part of each other, a part of the earth.

Salley McFague offers a way forward in her book, *Life Abundant*. She calls on Christians to participate with other traditions in an ecological reformation. She writes that "human beings are dependent on nature and responsible for it." This is what is meant by the word "subdue" in the passage above.

> All life grew from one cell into millions of species, into rich, diverse, and infinitely interesting forms we know–from mushrooms and mice to wheat and giant cedars, from fungi and frogs to chimpanzees and human beings. We are all related: We all came from the same beginning.[41]
>
> Sallie McFague

The Kindom of God is When

The Kindom of God, in Christian terms, is when human beings live the Three Great Teachings described in the Abrahamic tradition and written on the hearts of people everywhere. There are similar visions among many traditions. My friend Jay Bowen, an elder in the Upper Skagit Tribe, bore witness to the perspective of his people:

> When a spirit goes to earth, the Creator says three things to them–Enjoy yourself, help people, and don't hurt anyone.

Likewise, the core teachings of the Christian tradition offer a basis of ethical living and meaning for life. Western society has often offered that ever-increasing production and consumption are inherently more meaningful. This is a promise as empty as Christmas wrapping paper on December 26th. Our souls, our neighbors, our fellow creatures, and our earth cannot bear it any longer.

But we don't have to. Our ancient tradition offers, along with many other traditions, a way to experience meaning by living out the value of all creation, every person, and every community. This meaning may express itself by giving and receiving, in possibility and limits, and in humility and gratitude.

In 1993, Christian theologian Hans Küng called for people of all wisdom traditions to summarize a global ethic. He realized that while our traditions, stories, and practices differ, our ethics share much in common. Two hundred leaders at the Parliament of the World's Religions worked together and came up with this:

Commitment to a culture of

- non-violence and respect for life
- solidarity and a just economic order
- tolerance and a life of truthfulness
- equal rights and partnership between men and women

We are a part of one holy, good-and-very-good creation. In awe of life and the giver of life, we experience meaning in serving all of life and the blessings of the Kindom of God.

Chapter Sixteen: Story of Origin and Our Jewish Neighbors

We are all born to a world that has histories, strengths, and challenges. Dr. Martin Luther King taught that we are not responsible for the history we are born into. We are responsible to understand it and to make the future better.

Ehaab Abdu, a Zoroastrian and a scholar of Mesopotamian religions taught me about the many similarities and connections between these religions and those that developed around them. For instance, he suggested how similar the 42 Laws of Maat in Egyptian tradition are to the Ten Commandments.[42]

He gifted me with a painful and necessary realization: The way we tell the origin stories of our groups can dehumanize those who have come before and set us up to replicate the same problems.

Often, a new tradition emerges when a problem is not addressed by the widely held wisdom traditions of the day. To break away from a widely held wisdom tradition and begin a new one takes a lot of energy. So, we begin to draw distinctions between our new traditions and the existing ones. This is just fine.

The danger begins when we make false assumptions about these social problems:

- these problems are unique to these widely held traditions
- our new tradition will be immune to such problems
- all would be well if we just got rid of these traditions
- if our in-group and tradition solves the problem, we can't be a problem

When we tell our origin story this way, we sow the seeds of exclusive in-grouping that will later cause us to deny our own problems and dehumanize others.

While responsible wisdom traditions try to help us guard against our vulnerabilities and to amplify our positive potentialities, no tradition, no group, no society is immune to the vulnerabilities of human nature and domination culture. Every community of wisdom can distort its key values, stories, and practices to support a domination culture.

Ehaab helped me realize that I have spoken of the Egyptian and Mesopotamian religions in a dehumanizing way. While it was painful, I was grateful for his gift to me. How can I work against exclusive in-grouping and dehumanization by dehumanizing the traditions that came before? I have regularly done this toward Egyptian, Mesopotamian, Jewish, and many other traditions. Yes, there were social problems that they needed to address. Yes, it was okay for a new tradition to emerge to respond to these problems.

But, if the way we tell our stories of origin dehumanizes the wisdom traditions before us, we may use this prejudicial self-righteousness to absolve ourselves of looking at the ways our own tradition contributes to or blesses injustice. This move can sow seeds of supremacy that later grow and choke out much that is good in our own tradition. I will attempt to be careful as I speak of the story of origin of the Abrahamic tradition. As we saw earlier, respecting other traditions is in the deepest tradition of Abraham.

Supersessionism

In Sunday school, I was taught that Jesus came to start a new religion because Jewish people had been unfaithful to God. Jewish people have the "Old Testament," while Christians have the "New Testament." Jewish people have the old covenant, while Christians have the new covenant, which supersedes the old. This is called "supersessionism": the idea that God replaced and even negated the promises of God to Israelites with God's promises to Christians.

Supersessionism is the original exclusive in-grouping and dehumanization by Christians. But it didn't stop there. This dehumanization spread to Pagans, Muslims, Indigenous peoples, and many more.

Faithfulness in a Time of Crisis

Jesus grew up in a Jewish household. He learned the Torah's teachings. He learned the story of the Exodus by heart. He heard the words of the prophets, prayed the Psalms, and learned from the wisdom literature. He observed Shabbat and went to the local synagogue in Nazareth. He debated about the meaning of the Torah and the prophets with his family, his teachers, and his community as any faithful Jewish person does today. The Torah centers on this story:

> Then God spoke all these words: I am the Lord your
> God, who brought you out of the land of Egypt, out
> of the house of slavery.
> Exodus 20:1-2

The character of God is to love all the *mishpachah* in the world. When one of them is dehumanized, enslaved, or the victim of violence, God acts for their benefit by calling people to stand with each other.

Jesus makes it clear that his whole ministry flowed from this story, the Torah, and the prophets:

> Do not think that I have come to abolish the law
> or the prophets; I have come not to abolish but to
> fulfill. For truly I tell you, until heaven and earth
> pass away, not one letter, not one stroke of a letter,
> will pass from the law until all is accomplished.[43]
> Matthew 5:17-18

He was one of many leaders trying to discern how to be faithful within the crisis of occupation by the Roman Empire. Christians can claim that his approach was faithful. I think it's important to recognize that God may likely consider other leaders to have been faithful as well. The Abrahamic traditions remind us that only the Creator can judge such things.

What was the nature of the crisis?

The key narrative of the Hebrew tradition was liberation by God from enslavement from the domination culture within Egypt and Babylon. The Romans enforced a colonial form of enslavement: taking land, taking natural resources, brutally repressing any resistance, and limiting human rights for those who were not Roman citizens.

The Empire knew the story of liberation. They kept tight control of the Temple to keep this story of liberation as mere history. One example was that the Chief Priest's vestments were kept at the Governor's Palace. The message was clear: "Keep the story of liberation in the past, and you can keep your tradition. Apply it to the present, and another Chief Priest will need to be chosen due to your sudden, unfortunate death." Any wisdom tradition that can't be applied to the present is no longer a living tradition but a museum piece. Like many other leaders, Jesus looked to the Torah and prophets for a faithful response. In the Christian Scriptures, we see Jesus debating with others about what that faithful response might be.

In doing so, Jesus is not being Antisemitic. He is a member of a tradition and an in-group in a vigorous and contentious debate in a time of crisis. One such debate was about the purity codes around purifying hands:

> So the Pharisees and the scribes asked him, "Why do your disciples not live according to the tradition of the elders, but eat with defiled hands?" He said to them, "Isaiah prophesied rightly about you hypocrites, as it is written, 'This people honors me with their lips, but their hearts are far from me. In vain do they worship me teaching human precepts as doctrines.' You abandon the commandment of God and hold to human tradition."
> Mark 7:5-8

This was a vigorous debate! It is also a normal one for the time. How often do we debate each other about what is central and what is a distraction in our own traditions? All the time! (Actually, we are doing that right now in this book.) Ritually purifying hands helped the Jewish people maintain their in-group identity under Roman occupation. It enabled them to see each meal as holy. It allowed them to remember their identity as God's holy children through these daily spiritual practices.

Jesus' point, like that around the offering of sacrifices, was that washing hands is a spiritual practice. It was easy to focus on the practice and forget the deeper meaning: that we are part of a good and very good creation called to love each other and the earth. In this passage, Jesus repeats the words of Isaiah, who made this same critique.

But notice that the Israelites included these critiques in their scripture. They had the wisdom and humility to include their teachings (Torah and Wisdom), prayers (Psalms), and self-critiques (Prophets) in their sacred texts.

It is important for Christians to:

- learn from their capacity for self-critique
- not dehumanize Jewish people with their own self-critique
- apply those self-critiques to our tradition and community

Lastly, it is important to remember that Jesus was not rejecting his own wisdom tradition or his own people. Rather, his leadership focused on how to live out that tradition in response to the relentless, crushing pressure of the domination culture of the Roman Empire.

Our Original Dehumanization

Christians would do well to remember how our tradition held up under Constantine's takeover, the Doctrines of Discovery, the genocides of Indigenous peoples, and the enslavement of humans from Africa and beyond. How well have Christians done in caring for the earth? **Not. Well.**

> Or how can you say to your neighbor, "Let me take
> the speck out of your eye", while the log is in your
> own eye?
> Matthew 7:4

Jesus' critiques have often wrongly been used to dehumanize both the tradition, community, and genetic family of our Jewish neighbors. In this, Christians have failed the Abrahamic test: to be a blessing to all families, nations, cultures, and religions of the world. In this, we have dehumanized Jesus, Mary, Joseph, and the very tradition that Jesus led from and within. Centuries of violence have resulted.

Emerging in a Time of Occupation

The crisis of Roman occupation impacted how early Christianity developed.

First, the Roman Empire ruled by setting people against each other. They recognized only one inheritor of the Hebrew tradition. This pitted this new Jewish group, the early Christians, against the other Jewish groups.

Second, as the Christians were writing letters and gospels, they had to be careful how they talked about the Roman Empire. They had to use symbolic and poetic language to refer to Rome. They also sometimes blamed Jewish leadership for the death of Jesus. Let's be clear: **Jewish leadership did not have the power of capital punishment. Only the Roman Empire had that power.** The oppressive power of the empire prevented these writers from being explicit about the Empire. Under duress from the Empire they blamed Jesus' death on Jewish leaders and sometimes the whole of the Jewish people. We must root this out of the Christian tradition.

Third, as the early Christians gathered and the Romans pitted them against other Jewish groups, they tried to draw contrasts between themselves and their Jewish neighbors. Some of these contrasts were fine; others were dehumanizing of the Jewish community:

> For you, brothers and sisters, became imitators of
> the churches of God in Christ Jesus that are in Judea,
> for you suffered the same things from your own
> compatriots as they did from the [Judean Leaders",]
> who killed both the Lord Jesus and the prophets,
> and drove us out; they displease God and oppose
> everyone by hindering us from speaking to the
> Gentiles so that they may be saved. Thus they have
> constantly been filling up the measure of their sins;
> but God's wrath has overtaken them at last.
> First Thessalonians 2:14-16

It hurts me to write this. The Christian community and the Jewish community parted ways. No doubt, this created the sorrow and anger expressed in this passage. Christians, I believe, are called to take responsibility for passages like this and recognize them for what they are: Exclusive in-grouping and dehumanization that has led to violence against our Jewish neighbors. We are called to measure passages like this against the whole message of the Hebrew and Christian Scriptures. In doing so, we take scripture seriously. We are called to do a relentless inventory of our own tradition, including our Scripture, present attitudes and actions, and turn around from Antisemitism. Not only is Antisemitism an evil unto itself, but it has metastasized into many other forms of exclusive in-grouping.

In Sunday School, we were taught the song I Just Wanna Be a Sheep by Brian M. Howard.[44] I remember the leaders smiling and laughing while they taught it to us. As you read the song, notice that Jewish groups are mentioned in a song with animals and hypocrites.

I just wanna be a sheep
Baa, baa, baa, baa
I just wanna be a sheep
Baa, baa, baa, baa
I pray the Lord my soul to keep
Baa, Baa, Baa, Baa
I just wanna be a sheep
Baa, baa, baa, baa

Verse 1

Don't wanna be a goat, nope
Don't wanna be a goat, nope
Haven't got any hope, nope
Don't wanna be a goat, nope

Verse 2

Don't wanna be a hypocrite
Don't wanna be a hypocrite
'Cause they're not hip with it
Don't wanna be a hypocrite

Verse 3

Don't wanna be a Pharisee
Don't wanna be a Pharisee
'Cause they're not fair you see
Don't wanna be a Pharisee

Verse 4

Don't wanna be a Sadducee
Don't wanna be a Sadducee
'Cause they're so sad you see
Don't wanna be a Sadducee

Verse 5

Just wanna be a child of God
Just wanna be a child of God
Walk along the road He trod
Just wanna be a child of God

I remember laughing, too. I remember the dopamine hit of

superiority. The song is clever. But then dehumanization is often so. The rabbis of our modern day trace a part of their heritage to the Pharisees. The song links being a child of God, that is, being a part of our exclusive Christian in-group, with mocking those in an inferior in-group. Now I understand that we were the hypocrites we sang about.

Here is a story of the impact of Antisemitism on our Jewish neighbors:

> Mel Damski: Mine starts in fourth grade. My parents lived through the Holocaust. They grew up, they're from Berlin but they really wanted to protect us and they didn't want us to grow up with this heavy burden of Antisemitism and their personal history. They wanted us to be happy American kids. And a kid comes up to me in fourth grade at the East Hill School and he says, "You're a Christ-killer" and I said, "You're a Christ-killer." I had no idea what he was talking about, right? And I got home, and I said to my Father, "What was that all about?" And he explained to me this whole issue with the way Jews are perceived and how they were blamed for the death of Jesus and all of this. And it just opened up this world to me, that of the "other," the concept of the "other," because I never thought of myself as an "other."

As a child, Rabbi Levine, one of the founders of Paths to Understanding, heard people in the streets in Lithuania calling to "kill the Christ-killers." His response was not to dehumanize back but, instead, to stand with Roman Catholics when they were being dehumanized by creating the Challenge program in 1960 with William Warren of KOMO TV in Seattle, Washington.

We have much to learn from our Jewish siblings.

This original dehumanization has formed the basis within Christianity for the dehumanization of Muslim, Pagan, Indigenous, and many other communities. One dehumanization has begotten others. Today, the Pacific Northwest is one of the top three areas in the US in terms of the growth of hate crimes.

> Rabbi Daniel Weiner: I've had some wonderful teachers, both within the Jewish community and outside of the Jewish community, just in my secular studies, that

really helped me to understand, as is the case with so
many forms of prejudice, that education and expo-
sure and experience with different groups of people
is really the remedy if not the panacea for any kind of
hatred and any kind of stereotyping and bigotry but
particularly with Antisemitism. Hopefully, with again
a greater degree of education and a greater degree of
actual experience with Jews and other groups, that's
something that is classically known to mitigate things
like Antisemitism. It's not a guarantee, but it helps.

When we come together, get to know one another as neighbors,
share our traditions, and work for the common good together, we
begin to counter the dehumanizations that have harmed all of us.

White Nationalist Narrative

The dehumanization of our Jewish siblings has continued to develop and metastasize over the centuries. In this conversation with
Devin Burghart from the Institute for Research and Education on
Human Rights, we discussed the storyline of the White Nationalist
movement.

Terry Kyllo: What's the narrative that sort of ties all
this together. What are what are some of the stories,
the explanatory story for the world that many of
these groups are organizing themselves around?

Devin Burghart: That's a really good point to focus on. I
think there are a couple of different important things that
tie the far right in general together. The first is their ideological construct and it's what we've often described as a
kind of Middle-American Nationalism. It's the idea that
so-called Middle-American's either implicitly or explicitly
defined as White and Christian are being squeezed from
above by the elites which may or may not be defined
in an Antisemitic way oftentimes it is and from below
from the multicultural hordes or from the unproductive
those who are you know wanting to take and squeeze the
middle class and take away their rights and privileges
and their wealth so that's part of it right it is that idea
that there is a conspiracy between the elites and people

of color to deny the so-called Middle-American's their rightful place in society and their right to do what they want to do we certainly seen this play out writ-large during the pandemic and it was certainly part of the big thing that made trump so popular right that kind of idea ideological perspective runs throughout most of the far right today so that's one thing the second thing that's really important uh and that is so dominant is conspiratorial thinking right the idea that there is you know either the you know a secret cabal of the deep state who's out to you know gather up children and drink their blood for their the adrenochrome or it is the Bilderbergers or the Rothschilds or you know some other nefarious organization out there to control the levers of power to continue to turn that vice and squeeze that middle is really part of the conspiracy so we see that playing out today in so many different narratives right it's regurgitating age-old Antisemitic tropes around things like the blood libel and around you know the attacks on children so whether that is the you know the QAnon conspiracy theories or the attacks on critical race theory today or the attacks on trans folks and comprehensive sex education. The critique of these things so often today is coming from this conspiratorial thinking right it is a lack of a grounding in reason or empirical evidence. It is that based in fear that drives people to go to such extreme lengths today to engage in the kind of not just political campaigning but threats harassment intimidation and violence that we see so common as a part of the movement today.[45]

We saw this kind of narrative at work in the Pittsburgh Synagogue murderer. He was convinced by President Trump that there were caravans coming from Central America to steal from middle-class people. The local Jewish community offered services to refugees through the Hebrew Immigrant Aid Society. They help immigrants get started in life in their new nation.

He interpreted that false story about these caravans to mean (falsely):

- Jews are oppressing White people from above by supporting immigrants.
- The refugees were among those taking from and trying to replace White people from below.

He wrote this before he left his house:

> HIAS likes to bring invaders in that kill our people.
> I can't sit by and watch my people get slaughtered.
> Screw your optics, I'm going in.
> Pittsburgh Synagogue Murderer

You can see classic dehumanization at work here: He believed (falsely) that what he loved was being threatened by other groups. Thus, he had moral and even Divine approval for violence.

Words that harm lead to sticks and stones. These words are built on the sedimentary layers of exclusive in-grouping, dehumanization, and violence. This White Nationalist narrative in our nation began with the Antisemitic words within the Christian Scriptures, amplified by the takeover of Christianity by the Roman Empire, the Crusades, the Doctrines of Discovery, the genocide toward Indigenous peoples, the enslavement of human beings from Africa, and more.

All too often, Christian congregations are silent about this White Nationalist narrative and its terrible fruit. Our silence is interpreted as consent. I believe that Christians can learn from how we have contributed to this harm and to repent. In our baptismal identity, we are fully embraced and affirmed as we are and invited to do the joyful work of the healing and creation of the world.

Within the Abrahamic Tradition

It is a good thing that a new Abrahamic tradition formed in the crisis of Roman occupation. But Christians must remember that we are a part of a larger Abrahamic tradition whose core value is the blessing of all peoples, cultures, and traditions.

Many Christians are working hard to reform the Christian church in light of Jesus' 1st century, Jewish, Roman occupied context. While it is crucial for us to understand Jesus' Jewish tradition and his own take on Jewish teachings, we must refrain from making the mistake of supersessionism. To understand Jesus, we must understand 1st century Judaism. But it is simply not acceptable to understand Judaism through Jesus. Christianity became a distinct tradition. Judaism remains its own tradition, even if we are related in the larger Abrahamic tradition. All too often, Christians impose our understanding of Jesus' teachings on our Jewish neighbors. This toxic expression of supersessionism powers Christian exclusive in-grouping and denies the voice of our Jewish neighbors to describe their own tradition. It keeps Christians from hearing our Jewish neighbors and functions to increase the social distance from and violence toward them.

When our traditions differ, we can take a cue from our Muslim neighbors:

> For each of you (nations) we have appointed a
> law and a way. And had God willed, God would
> have made you one community, but God willed
> otherwise, that God might test you in what God has
> given you. So vie with each other in good deeds.
> Unto God shall be your return all together, and God
> will inform you over what you used to differ.
> Holy Quran 5:48

It is also true that Christians must grow in their capacity to recognize that other Abrahamic traditions are connected to us, are a part of the larger tradition, and have distinct teachings and practices. Rabbi Levine challenged Father Treacy, a Catholic priest, to understand the Jewish roots of his tradition. Father Treacy learned to recognize those roots and to see the Jewish tradition as a distinct but related tradition.

A professor at the seminary taught us that we are free to read the Hebrew scripture and to see it in Christian terms. But we must remember that we are, in a sense, borrowing it. We can be more faithful to Jesus when we listen, as he did, to the reflections of our own Jewish neighbors. We can also learn to debate the core values of the Abrahamic tradition respectfully with all members of Abraham's family.

Kay Knott, an elder in the Upper Skagit Tribe, shared that in her tradition, the Creator has spoken to every tribe around the world in the way each needs.

Perhaps we can grow in gratitude for our siblings in faith and be grateful with them for the grace of the Creator to each of us in our own context and time. Perhaps we can still, even after all our challenges, live more fully into the promise of the Abrahamic tradition.

Chapter Seventeen: Practice of Love

Wisdom traditions offer us ways of moving about in the world and making decisions in real time that reflect our deep values. They help us learn from previous generations and, sometimes, our own contribution may be shared with future generations to help them live in the wisdom of love.

Wisdom traditions often condense this wisdom in images (like a cross, the Star of David, or the statue of Buddha) and some important words. We can carry these words and pictures in our heads and hearts. But there is a danger in putting so much meaning into a few symbols or words. If someone twists the meaning of those words, the entire tradition can go astray and even begin to support a domination culture.

Willingness to Risk

Two of the most important words in the Abrahamic traditions are "love" and "neighbor."

In the Christian Scriptures, the Greek word for love is *agape*. It means "risking love." Greek had other words for other forms of love, but the writers of the Gospels used *agape* to represent what Jesus means by "love."

Agape is the willingness to risk time, money, effort, reputation, relationships, and even (under certain circumstances) our physical safety to enhance the well-being of ourselves, our neighbors, our neighborhoods, and the ecosystem.

In Christian terms, then, love is risking with others to work toward the coming of the Kindom of God in the world.

Christians have often distorted the meaning of love by reducing it to warm feelings and nice thoughts. Some Christians have distorted love to mean converting other people using manipulation so they can go to heaven when they die.

The idea of neighbor is usually distorted by categorizing who is and who is not my neighbor, who is human and who is not, and/or ranking people in terms of worth.

There are many examples of how Christians distorted the idea of neighbor. One was in the Nazi era:

> The failure of the church in the Nazi era was obviously an activist failure, a failure to do. But prior to that, it was more fundamentally a failure to see–to see the Jews as those with whom Christians were called to be. The parable of the Last Judgement is often interpreted as a call to activism, but it is more fundamentally an identification of those the church is called to be with.
> Sam Wells

In other words, the Christian Church in Germany failed to act in love for their Jewish neighbors because they didn't have deep, respectful, public relationships with them. Social distance between people of diverse wisdom traditions and cultures is not neutral. It sets the stage for dehumanization and violence. The social distance between the more powerful German Christians and their Jewish neighbors contributed to the Holocaust.

Social connections between groups can reduce the possibility of violence. The Omnia Center for Contextual Leadership is creating connections between wisdom communities in many countries around the world. These intergroup connections have prevented violence.

We saw a similar dynamic in Hawaii when Japanese Incarceration was ordered by the US Government in Executive Order 9066. While Japanese Americans were losing their property, businesses, and freedom in Japanese Incarceration, they did not experience this in Hawaii. Why? Because they had deep and wide connections with diverse groups in Hawaii. When the order came down, the community leaders made it clear to the military that concentration camps would not be allowed.

When we read the Gospels, we see Jesus consistently risking himself for the Kindom of God and recognizing people as neighbors by being in public relationship with them. He refused to let the Roman Empire keep him from fellow humans. In doing so, he wasn't just being nice. He understood what Rabbi Levine understood: **Honoring our common humanity is the precondition of our survival.**

Who Are We Called to Be With?

The Gallup Organization tracks racial segregation. They found that Sunday morning is the most segregated time of the week. This reveals that Christian communities are not only isolated from people of other wisdom traditions but from Christians of different cultures and ethnic backgrounds.[46]

Ervin Staub survived the Nazis because his Polish babysitter claimed him as her son. His Jewish family were largely victims of genocide. In honor of her, he studies why genocides happen and how to prevent them.

His conditions for genocide include:

- cultural self-concept
  - superiority
  - self-doubt/persecution
- difficult life conditions
- longstanding racism[47]

We can see much of this across the world and in the United States. But we are not powerless. Through his research, Staub has discovered that when people in the majority relate to, stand with, and stand behind minorities early in the process of dehumanization, we can interrupt genocide.

> Opposition (to dehumanization) from bystanders,
> whether based on moral or other grounds, can
> change the perspective of perpetrators and other
> bystanders, especially if the bystanders act at an
> early point on the continuum of destruction.
> Ervin Staub

We are seeing a frightful rise in dehumanizing speech toward minorities and between political parties. We are seeing the fruit of that in a rise in hate crimes and political violence.

Wisdom traditions offer us collected wisdom. But they also offer something else. At their best, wisdom traditions retain the memory of how people in our community have failed to live our values. This can equip us to behave differently when similar circumstances arise.

Well, here we are.

Let's Go Together and other efforts are about gathering as diverse a group as possible to eat and share stories, work for the common good, and stand together in public. This book is a preparation for Christians for this kind of public partnership. It is preparation for action.

When we develop relationships across lines of difference, both as individuals and as communities of wisdom, we move from being passive bystanders to active leaders.

Beyond Thoughts and Prayers

At a nice church one morning, a woman said: "I have never felt that way about Muslims or Jews." She was responding to a list of anti-Muslim and Antisemitic ideas spread by hate groups.

I responded: "Your Muslim and Jewish neighbors don't care what you think. What they want to know is whether you will be in relationship with them and stand with them when they need you."

Our attitudes do matter. But when our love for people is expressed only in yelling at the TV, posting on social media, or only talking about it in church, then love doesn't make much difference. For Christians, love is something not simply to feel but to practice.

> Now large crowds were travelling with him; and he turned and said to them, "Whoever comes to me and does not hate father and mother, wife and children, brothers and sisters, yes, and even life itself, cannot be my disciple. Whoever does not carry the cross and follow me cannot be my disciple. For which of you, intending to build a tower, does not first sit down and estimate the cost, to see whether he has enough to complete it?"
> Luke 14:25-28

Jesus isn't asking us to "emotionally hate" our family. People in the 1st century Mediterranean world were deeply constrained by the expectations of their family and community. These expectations were often very good ones for which all of us would strive.

The word "hate" in this context has to do with reputation. Sometimes, living out love for our neighbors requires us to break family and societal expectations. Jesus is suggesting that, in his context, people would have to risk their reputations, relationships, and, possibly, their personal safety to live out love of all neighbors.

I want to be clear. Living out love for all our neighbors by being in relationship, working together, and standing in public will be risky.

When I told my home congregation that I was no longer serving a congregation but rather countering the dehumanization of my Muslim neighbors, most of them could not look at me. I have lost friends. I have experienced distance from some family. I have been told that I am a traitor to Jesus, the country, and God. Others have told me that I am a fool for spending time on something that I cannot solve. Others want to reduce me to my work, holding me up to standards I cannot live up to and then judging me when I am just a human being. I have felt, at times, endangered physically. For about six months, I could not speak in public without a glass of water since my body was having a stress reaction.

But then I realized that my Muslim, Black, Indigenous, Jewish, and many other neighbors deal with this stress every single day. They are examples to me of how to hold this risk and how to let it go. They helped me realize that our mutual well-being is at stake. After much prayer and conversation my body's stress reaction lessened.

You will risk things, too. It is important for you to count the cost before you begin. It is even more important to become clear about why. The activities for this chapter found on our website, are intended to help you become clearer about your "why." To know your "why" is powerful for your ongoing energy, and for your response to others.

A few years ago, I spoke to a man at my home church. He asked how my work was going. He told me that he had thought a lot about what I was doing. He was concerned about the divisions in the society and how we are speaking of each other. He told me that while he had more to learn about Muslims, and still had some trust issues that they deserved the same rights as every other American.

But we don't do this work just because it may have a good effect. We certainly don't do it to enter the "risk Olympics." Our best calling is our authentic calling. We do this work because we are human, **and** we recognize each other as human.

Here again is Father William Treacy, one of our founders, from the original Challenge program in 1972:

Father William Treacy: Could Christ be crucified in

the United States, for example, in 1972? Who cruci-fied Christ? It is only fitting that here, in the garden where he was arrested, that we recall an event that took place in a central city in the eastern part of the United States last year on Good Friday, the anniver-sary day that Christians recall Christ's death. Priests and people began with a procession to the down-town district to one of the poorest areas of the city.

And there, a priest made this statement: "In buildings as you see around you, unscrupulous landlords con-demned Christ to death by charging high rent for poor, inadequate housing which resulted in poor education, poor health care, and exploitation by dope-pushers and by gamblers. The procession then went to the down-town business section with its large office buildings for so many times a profit motive had guided policy at the expense of the environment, at the expense of hu-man dignity, and of justice. The last scene took place before the city morgue, where a prayer was recited for a derelict who had died that day on Skid Row, the vic-tim of alcoholism and neglect by society. The service concluded with these words of Jesus: As long as you did it for one of my least brothers, you did it for me."

What is our responsibility for slums and the exploitation of human beings, for indifference to the environment and human values, for crime and its victims, for war and its tragic consequences? And the answer to these questions is the answer to the question: Who cruci-fied Christ? Remember, he said, as long as you did it for one of these, my least brothers, you did it for me.

The Abrahamic tradition teaches that we are made in the image of a Creator who longs to bless all the families, nations, and reli-gions of the world—the *mishpachah* of the world. We are meant to be different, and we are meant to be one. As we grow in relationship with each other, we experience the life that God intends for us. As we honor the humanity of others, we find our own. We bless, and we are blessed by each other, and by the God of infinite blessings.

Chapter Eighteen: The Meaning of Sacrifice

Some Christians resist respecting and working together with people of diverse traditions and cultures because of how they understand Jesus' death on the cross. They have been taught that forgiveness and acceptance from God is only available through Jesus. For them, this means that no other tradition is valid. So, they focus on converting others to their version of Christianity.

This is only one way to understand the meaning of Jesus' death on the cross. This way of understanding the meaning of Jesus' death was made possible because Christians lost, within 100 years, our connection to the theological tradition of the Jewish people.

We will begin to understand the meaning of Jesus' death on the cross through a conversation with Rabbi Daniel Weiner of Temple de Hirsch Sinai in Seattle, Washington. Then, we will go on to explore the meaning of sacrifice and a biblical view of the meaning of Jesus' public, painful death.

A Conversation Between Rabbi Weiner and Pastor Terry Kyllo

> Terry Kyllo: I'm so happy to welcome today and to be in conversation with Rabbi Danny Weiner, who's the senior rabbi at Temple De Hirsch Sinai in Seattle, the temple where Rabbi Raphael Levine, one of the founders of Paths to Understanding, served for many years. Danny, thank you so much for being in conversation with me about the whole idea of sacrifice. And we've got a number of questions here, and I just appreciate your time today.

> Rabbi Danny Weiner: It's my honor and pleasure. I feel so blessed to be the successor to Rabbi Levine and Father Treacy's work and the work that you are so critically facilitating moving forward. So please, it's a joy.

> Terry Kyllo: Thank you. Thank you so much,

Danny. So today, there are so many people who
are setting aside traditions, blaming traditions
and communities of wisdom in general for all of
our problems. Why is a tradition important?

Rabbi Danny Weiner: I think a tradition is important
because it is profoundly grounding. As much as I am
a supporter of the freedoms of our liberal democracy,
at times, they can be a little bit too focused on the individual. And this notion of a tradition that connects
you to ideas and, people and places both in time and in
space is really critical. I think what it is to live a healthy,
ethical, moral life, spiritually, psychologically, etcetera,
is really to find that balance between the traditions, the
gifts of wisdom and insight that we have inherited from
those who came before us, with a need to respond to
modern sensibilities and modern needs. And so I think
with tradition, like everything in life, moderation and
finding that middle ground is really important. Too
much individualism, and we're all disconnected. Too
much tradition, and there is not a responsiveness to
the changing sensibilities of our contemporary times.

Terry Kyllo: Thank you. Thank you so much. So Danny,
in the last especially 40 years, but maybe just a bit longer,
Christians have begun to reckon with the reality that by
the end of the 1st century, that many Christian teachers
and writers were no longer Jewish and had really lost
touch with the Hebrew Scriptures as well as the culture of
1st century Israel, a culture in which Jesus was living and
leading and having conversations. So part of the conversation today is to ask, what are the ancient origins of sacrificing an animal to God as far as we can know it today?

Rabbi Danny Weiner: So probably one of the most
primitive kinds of pre-Jewish notions or pre-Israelite,
excuse me, that's a better way of describing it, pre-
Israelite notions from the ancient Near East was really
feeding and assuaging the God or the gods. You had a
great hunt, that was not something that you took for
granted. And so you would make an offering of part

of your bounty to the gods, or God or whomever, as a way of thanking nature for having provided something that they didn't really take for granted. Judaism, the early Israelite religion, really built upon that but took it in a very different direction. And the main direction had to do with our understanding of what those sacrifices, what those offerings meant to God.

From a Jewish perspective, God does not need our sacrifices. The sacrifices are far more about the transformation that takes place within the person who is giving the sacrifice, both the individual transformation personal transformation, but also the transformation of a larger society that takes place through that giving beyond oneself thinking and being aware of the needs of those beyond oneself. And from our theological understanding in Judaism, God doesn't need animals. God doesn't need sacrifices. God certainly transcends need, let alone the need for things. The why God requests this, why God commands this from an ancient Israelite point of view, is to render a profound transformation and broadening of scope for us.

Terry Kyllo: Yeah, that's really wonderful to hear. And I first came across this idea when I was in seminary through the writing of a biblical scholar named Lawrence Boadt who wrote, and this was just in my seminary introduction to the Hebrew scripture class, that the Hebrew people, unlike many of those around them at the time, did not really think that their sacrifices changed God, which seems arrogant that we could do something that would change God's heart or character toward us. But sadly, I think what has happened, and it's largely through the writing of one guy named Anselm of Canterbury, who, in the 11th century, was almost completely unaware of the Hebrew tradition around sacrifice. And he was a feudal lord. As feudal lord, anybody born on his property basically belonged to him.

And so he used that as a metaphor for Christianity and basically saying that we owe the creator obedience, but you can't be extra obedient. You're either obedient, or you're not. And so if you sin against your Lord, well then there's no possible forgiveness for it because then the whole futile system would break down. And so it requires some kind of payment or some kind of punishment, and then the idea that Jesus provides that payment through the cross and so on. And so many Christians really struggle with this. So again, what you're saying is that in the Hebrew tradition, it was distinct from other, some other traditions saying that God doesn't really need sacrifice. I mean, that's really different for many Christians to contemplate.

Rabbi Danny Weiner: No, absolutely. In terms of what you're saying about Anselm, I'm reminded of that old Mark Twain phrase that God created man, and man returned the favor. In other words, it's not surprising that Anselm, just from his narrow scope of how the world worked for him, felt that that would be a model or a template to apply to the cosmos and the universe. The Hebrew word for sacrifice or for an offering is *corban*. And *corban* comes from the Hebrew root meaning to draw near, to bring closer. And so inherent in that sense that yes, it is a, in some ways in the immediate moment, a one-way offering. It really is about bringing the worshiper closer to God and, even more importantly, bringing the worshiper closer to other people in the community.

Because logistically speaking, the sacrifices, and I'm over-generalizing, but it's basically this, were divided into three parts. One part would go to the poor in the community, one part would go to the priestly class and their families because their full-time gig was running the temple, they weren't out raising animals or farming, and then a part of it was burned on an altar to God. But it's that part that was burned onto an altar to God, which really, I think in many ways, symbolically and motivationally undergirded the first two that is supporting the sacrificial system, but most importantly, heightening awareness and motivating offerings to those in need within the community.

Terry Kyllo: Right. In the Hebrew scripture, there's a number of passages. Some of them seem to suggest that sacrificing is absolutely essential in some way, and there's other ones that are a critique of that idea. So in Exodus 20, "You need make for me only an altar of earth and sacrifice your burnt offerings and your offerings of wellbeing, your sheep and your oxen. In every place where I cause my name to be remembered, I will come to you and bless you." And that's an example of the necessity or the importance of sacrifice, perhaps. And then there's many others, including Isaiah chapter six, verse six, "For I desire steadfast love and not sacrifice, the knowledge of God rather than burnt offerings." So can you help us understand from the broad Jewish perspective these two seemingly disparate statements?

Rabbi Danny Weiner: Absolutely. Looking at it from the point of view of the biblical period, the prophetic critique of the sacrificial system once it was established, the prophets were basically saying the prophets were recognizing that people were missing the forest for the trees. They were getting so bogged down in a punctilious fidelity to the details of the sacrifices that they lost the train of thought to truly understand and appreciate that the sacrifices were a means to an end, not an end in and of themselves. The point of the sacrifices was to get to the values and ethics behind the sacrifices. And today, my branch of Judaism has taken that to the next level and said, "We resonate with the prophetic message because today, people get so hung up on ritual that they forget that the ritual is a means to an end to the values and ethics and morality that lies beneath."

So the prophetic critique was really saying, "Look, don't feel like your entire duty's to God. Your worship of God has been discharged because you've gone through the motions." Unless your heart and your actions based on that changed heart align with the point of what those sacrifices are supposed to intend, you're not only missing the point, but it's like an ultimate insult to God and to the community because your intention is just to check off things on a laundry list, not to actually change one's heart, and one's mind, and one's actions. In terms of the Exodus text, one of the things that's really critical to understand about Jewish history and what makes that intertestamental period, that period between the closing out of the Jewish scriptures and the New Testament, is that that was a dramatic and transformative period, not only in terms of Jesus and the advent of Christianity but also the destruction of the temple in 70 CE by the Romans.

The destruction of the Second Temple in Jerusalem was meant to be, and it was a catastrophic event. And the Romans and other imperial forces did these kinds of things to destroy a national cultural, religious and political center as a way of undermining that whole society and absorbing them into the greater empire. Now, that should have happened to the Jewish people. However, they were able to do something pretty significant. They were able to maintain a connection to the transcendent values of Judaism while changing significantly and dramatically the way Judaism was practiced.

In other words, instead of a central temple, suddenly, you had local synagogues throughout the community. Instead of a sacrificial system that was based on animal sacrifice and fire and flame and blood, sacrifice became verbal and became the work, the worship of the heart, not the worship of the material offerings. And instead of priests being the main authoritative body based on their understanding of the sacrificial system, you had rabbis who based their understanding on the interpretation of scripture. And so Judaism did something incredibly clever, and it's really, the only reason why it survived is that it was able to radically change, modify, and adapt to the changing circumstances of a life without the temple while at the same time staying connected to the profound values that undergirded Judaism from its earliest stages.

Terry Kyllo: Right. So, the point of sacrifice was really to offer something of value. In this case, our heart, our intentions, our prayers, our time to be in community, our ability to love our neighbor around us and take care of those who are hurting in this moment or maybe are poor in this moment, but to do the act of sacrificing that to the Creator partly in gratitude for the gift of life that we're all experiencing here together.

Rabbi Danny Weiner: Yeah, the psychospiritual bottom line here is if you can make room in your consciousness for God and things bigger than yourself, and certainly something as august as God, how much more so hopefully can you broaden your narrow perspective on the world beyond yourself and your kin and encompass the greater good of the society in which you live?

Terry Kyllo: Right. Which brings us back to the first question: really, what's a tradition for? Is it to lift up some values that are really important, that we're willing to sacrifice for, values that we're willing to hold ourselves accountable to, stories that help encourage us, and to understand how to live those values in the real world in real-time? And then over time, to be able to look at ourselves and say, "Well, hey, this is what we said that was important to us, and did we do that?" And to hold ourselves accountable? For that, which, of course, is what the prophetic tradition in the Hebrew scripture is all about, is a community holding itself accountable.

And I think, to some degree, Christianity is trying to rediscover that prophetic tradition about ourselves. How should we hold ourselves accountable to our stated ideals? After so many centuries where, after the emperor Constantine essentially took over Christianity, I think we really had, not the conversion of the empire, but the conversion of Christianity to support empire. And we're still trying to recover from that and even identify the many ways in which that has impacted our prayers, our liturgies, our worship, our songs, our theology, our understanding of the Hebrew scripture, and our understanding of the Christian Scriptures.

Rabbi Danny Weiner: I could not have put it better myself, but I would not dare have spoken outside of my bailiwick here.

Terry Kyllo: Well, Danny, thank you so much for taking this time to be in conversation with us and the folks that are watching this video, and we just so appreciate your leadership and your friendship as well.

Rabbi Danny Weiner: It's my honor and pleasure. And thank you for all that you do, and look forward to continuing our work together to respond to the needs of a troubled moment.

Chapter Nineteen: The Sacrifice I Desire

After almost every public event where I appeared with Muslims to counter anti-Muslim bigotry, someone said the same thing: "You should be converting Muslims to Christianity so that God can forgive them and then they can go to heaven."

Under this statement is the assumption that God cannot forgive human beings without sacrifice, specifically the sacrifice of Jesus. This is one of the biggest hindrances among many Christians for respecting and working with people of diverse wisdom traditions.

Practice as Preparation

My family didn't have a lot of financial resources when I was a child. But since my Father was the custodian of the school, we had a key to the gym. After working for ten to eleven hours, my Father would take me to the gym and practice basketball with me. We had dribbling, passing, and shooting drills. We practiced both right hand and left hand—in fact, often twice as much with my left hand. These were holy times.

The purpose of practice is to gain skills for playing the game. While being an average natural athlete, I became a very good high school player. I learned a lot about myself, others, and life playing basketball. Good coaches know that any sport is about learning about life. Some coaches forget this.

Some forget this in wisdom traditions, too.

Every tradition has spiritual practices. Some are individual, others are communal. Some are private, and some public. The purpose for these practices is to help us prepare to live life in the real world and in real time.

We use spiritual practices to integrate various aspects of human experience: mind, emotions, spirit, body, relationships, and the creation. We often work the hardest at things that come the hardest to us. Muslims bow to the ground to physically experience total vulnerability to and trust in the Creator. Buddhists seek to quiet their minds and give up unhealthy attachments through the practice of meditation. Jewish congregations gather to recognize how we all miss the mark of love and to find a new beginning. Sikh communities gather around their sacred text that embodies the teachings of the Guru so that they can embody them in their lives. Some Indigenous communities taught people to bathe in the river every day in the winter, to cleanse themselves to become their best selves with the teaching of their elders. Christians eat and drink the Lord's Supper, recognizing that we participate in the body of Christ in the world.

These practices prepare us for life. How we do them matters. Each tradition has many teachings about how to do these practices. These teachings represent the lived wisdom of generations. These practices prepare us for connection to the divine, to that which is beyond us and beyond our definition. They prepare us to experience awe at the life we have been given. As important as the practices are, they are not themselves "the thing." They are preparation for life and for connection to the divine and one another.

Sacrifice

As Rabbi Daniel Weiner said, sacrifice is a means to an end. In other words, **sacrifice was a spiritual practice** meant to foster a community of justice and peace. It was both a gift to honor the Creator and a gift to the basic needs of the community. What many think is the standard view of the meaning of Jesus' death does not fit the understanding of sacrifice in the Scriptures.

In the book of Hosea, God says:

> For I desire steadfast love and not sacrifice,
> the knowledge of God rather than burnt offerings.
> Hosea 6:6

The People of Israel understood that sacrifice does not change God. Instead, sacrifice is giving up something of value to honor the value of all life and the One Creator. God does not need sacrifices. In Psalms, God says:

> If I were hungry, I would not tell you,
> for the world and all that is in it is mine.
> Psalm 50:12

When the community fell short of practicing the true meaning of sacrifice, truth-tellers were sent to set the record straight. Practice is for the game, not an end in itself.

> To do righteousness and justice
> is more acceptable to God than sacrifice.
> Proverbs 21:3

God forgives because God desires to. Sacrifice might help people recognize it, feel it, and experience it. But God chooses to be reconciled with us:

> I, I am the One
> who blots out your transgressions for my own
> sake,
> and I will not remember your sins.
> Isaiah 43:25

Forgiveness for sin and reaching out to be reconciled to human beings is God's character, it is a choice that God makes. Sacrifice was one way for one community, the People of Israel, to experience it. But the Creator has the freedom to seek the same goal of reconciliation differently with people in different cultures. The Creator is always free.

Lost Meaning

As we have noted earlier, by the end of the 1st century, Christians lost contact with the Hebrew tradition and the Roman-occupied cultural context of Jesus' ministry. The Gospel writers assumed that their texts would be read by people who knew their culture. The loss of our understanding of the original context meant a loss of the intended meanings of the text. We cannot ever be totally certain of their meanings. Still, a greater understanding of the original contexts can, at least, get us within a reasonable range.

The meaning of sacrifice was lost very early in Christian history. Once lost, it was interpreted in ways far different than in the Hebrew scripture. In the 11th century, Anselm of Canterbury, a feudal lord, used that system of domination as a metaphor for Jesus' sacrifice. Sadly, it has become the default understanding among many Christians:

- we owe the Creator obedience
- we do not obey and so incur a debt of sin to God

- we cannot make up for our debt of sin
- God is "just" and requires payment for this debt
- God sent Jesus, who paid our sin debt
- now the sin bookkeeping department is happy
- we can get in on this amnesty if we take Jesus as our personal Lord and Savior

In Anselm's day, the Middle Ages, this made a lot of sense to people struggling with a common anxiety: How can we find forgiveness in a God who is angry at human sin? Anselm's theory gave them a way to understand that Jesus took care of their debt of sin, and the church gave them ways to experience this forgiveness. This theory worked for them because it took their economic and social reality and added a twist of grace. No feudal lord would ever give a son to forgive the debt of a serf. But Anselm said that God had done just that. It helped them to understand one of the things that the church had always said Jesus did: offer forgiveness to human beings.

However popular it became in the Middle Ages and today, there are many problems with his theory. Some of these did not go unnoticed in Anselm's day. Most problematic is that Anselm's theory misunderstands God's character by saying:

- God cannot forgive
- God needs violence to forgive
- God approves of human sacrifice

These assumptions counter the very clear message of scripture: God's character is compassion and mercy:

> The Lord passed before Moses, and proclaimed,
> "The Lord, the Lord,
> a God merciful and gracious,
> slow to anger,
> and abounding in steadfast love and faithfulness"
> Exodus 34:6

God does not need violence to forgive:

> Jesus said: "Go and learn what this means, 'I desire mercy, not sacrifice.' For I have come to call not the righteous but sinners."
> Matthew 9:13

God never approves of or asks for child sacrifice:

> And (my people) go on building the high place
> of Topheth, which is in the valley of the son of
> Hinnom, to burn their sons and their daughters in
> the fire—which I did not command, nor did it come
> into my mind.
> Jeremiah 7:31

Anselm set the tone for much of Western Christianity. Based on his unbiblical theory of the meaning of sacrifice, we have concluded that Jesus is a limited offer of love and forgiveness only available to Christians (and often only a certain kind). We make Jesus into a mascot for our exclusive in-group.

But, if Anselm got it wrong, how do we understand Jesus' life, death, and resurrection?

Risking Life for Love of Life

When firefighters go into a burning house, they are risking and offering their lives to save lives. Many understand that the Creator has called them to this work of saving lives. They do it because they value the lives of the people inside the house.

Jesus risked his life. He sacrificed his time, energy, reputation, and, yes, his life.

Why?

The Roman Empire used state-sponsored terror to maintain their rule. The cross was both the summit and the symbol of this terror. They crucified thousands of people a year near the entrances to major cities. It was painful. It was humiliating–to the person, to their family, and to the whole nation. Through crucifixion, the Romans announced that they had power and that others had none. Through crucifixion, the Romans announced that the Kingdom of Rome was forever, and no other kingdom could take root.

Jesus knew that his revolution of love in the Kindom of God was a threat to the empire. He knew that his leadership would mean that he would be crucified. He trusted that he would be raised from the dead–thus emptying the cross of its power to intimidate people into silence and complicity. In the resurrection, the Creator redefines the end of the story. Life wins. Love wins. A new Kindom is possible, even inevitable.

They went on from there and passed through
Galilee. He did not want anyone to know it; for he
was teaching his disciples, saying to them, "The Son
of Man is to be betrayed into human hands, and they
will kill him, and three days after being killed, he
will rise again."

Mark 9:30-31

His death on a cross and his resurrection meant that his followers, while living under Rome, were no longer of Rome: no longer
enslaved to the sin of domination but freed to love themselves and
their neighbors. Jesus endured the cross to free people from the
power of domination, its symbol, the cross, and fear it produced.
His resurrection meant they could live the life the Creator wanted
for all people. In Jesus, they encountered forgiveness for going
along with domination and found a new beginning.

In Romans chapters six through eight, Paul writes that Jesus' disciples were free to live into the Kindom of God. No threat, no fear,
and no power could stop them. Disciples of Jesus joined into his
death had already died. They died to the status-keeping system,
the need to dominate and compete, the need to create exclusive in-
groups, and dehumanize others. They had already been raised, so
the power of the use of death by the Romans (or anyone else) could
no longer enslave them to participate in destructive ways of life.
Jesus didn't "have to die on the cross" to appease God. He died to
show his people that while the Roman empire was destroying human beings and distorting people's humanity through crucifixion,
they could begin to live the Kindom of God in the here and now.

Jesus risked his life. He sacrificed his life. He gave his valuable
life because people and the creation are beautiful and valuable.
Like a firefighter, he ran into a burning building to save lives, to
free people to live the life that the Creator intends. He learned this
from his own tradition, from his mother and father, from his teachers, and from his own spiritual practices in the Jewish tradition.

Jesus turned the symbol of terror and fear into a symbol of love
and courage. Like a firefighter going into a burning building, he
understood that his calling of love included taking this risk–not
because God could not forgive people or love them otherwise. Because God already loved them. They were trapped in fear in a bullying culture that used the state-sponsored terror of the cross. God
wanted to free them. Jesus experienced the cross. Jesus' resurrection

was a sign and symbol that they were free from that terror. The Creator works to free us still from whatever holds us back. We are free to love all of life and the Creator, to love ourselves and our neighbors, and to create a just economy and a thriving ecosystem.

And yes, through Jesus, his followers experienced forgiveness, a new direction, and a new beginning. In Jesus, the character of God is revealed to Christians as a God who is full of mercy, compassion, and steadfast love. To honor beings created in the image of God is to cultivate this character in ourselves.

Jesus sacrificed his life, the best, most valuable thing he had, so we might recognize the value of our own lives and find the courage to honor all of life as the Creator intends.

Then, he asked us to risk ourselves in our own contexts to reflect the power of God to free us and our neighbors for the life the Creator envisions.

> Then he said to them all, "If any want to become my followers, let them deny themselves and take up their cross daily and follow me."
> Luke 9:23

All because life is beautiful and worth protecting.

Chapter Twenty: Why Do We Do Domination?

Great traditions offer insights about human nature: What we are vulnerable to and what we are capable of. These insights are about both individuals and about societies. They are offered so that we can identify and minimize our vulnerabilities and maximize our potential.

Christians often use the word "sin" to talk about both the vulnerabilities of human nature and specific harmful behaviors that harm us, others, or creation.

In this all-too-brief chapter, I am mostly addressing the first as it sets the table for the second.

Before we go on, take a moment to examine how your body feels when you read the word "sin." Notice how you feel, physically and emotionally.

Here, I share what I have learned so far.

The Cow Pie

When I was a child, I heard the church say that I was basically bad. This was somehow both my own fault and an inescapable part of being human. Only through Jesus could I escape this terrible condition and its ever-after consequences. I call this a cow pie theology. Humans are cow pies out in the field. Jesus is like whipped cream that can cover up our destroyed goodness. The whipped cream of Jesus covers but does not get to the heart of the cow pie. This understanding of sin used to make my body feel cold and numb and my stomach full of pain.

I was taught that all humans are in this situation and Jesus is the only way for us to escape judgment and hell. Therefore, other traditions and cultures are expressions of sin or, at best, a false path. People of all traditions and cultures must be converted–not worked with, respected, and honored. In my experience, much of the conversation about sin was used to shame and bully. Ironically, this conversation of sin was itself full of sin, as I understand it now.

In response to this cow pie vision of human beings, others reject the idea of sin altogether. In doing so, they miss out on some key insights. Early in my ministry, I heard many Baby Boomers tell me that we were finally "over sin" and a better world was inevitable. Many of these good people are now passive and despairing in the face of our collective challenges.

You Will Be Like God

I had breakfast with Theologian Douglas John Hall one day. He is among the theologians who have shaped my current perspectives. He was teaching at a conference, and my friend Red Burchfield encouraged me to sit at his table with him. I had never met him before. Red is a troublemaker, but the good kind. He said, "John, Terry has some interesting thoughts about the Creeds." Dr. Hall looked at me and said, "I'd like to hear them." I swallowed hard.

"The core message of the creed is this: "If being human is good enough for God in Jesus, then it is good enough for us."

John said to me: "Yea, verily."

We then went on to talk about other matters, having addressed the Creed and the heart of Christianity, at least for breakfast time. "Yea, verily" is the King James translation of "yes, truly."

We are all tempted to reject life-as-it-is which includes:

- life and death
- possibility and failure
- health and sickness
- potential and vulnerability
- power and weakness

Life-as-it-is includes "both sides of the coin" of these realities. We see this in the second story of creation in Genesis 2-3.

> But the serpent said to the woman, 'You will not die;
> for God knows that when you eat of it your eyes will
> be opened, and you will be like God, knowing good
> and evil. So when the woman saw that the tree was
> good for food, and that it was a delight to the eyes,
> and that the tree was to be desired to make one wise,
> she took of its fruit and ate; and she also gave some
> to her husband, who was with her, and he ate.
> Genesis 3:4-6

The first humans, representing all humans, ate the fruit because they wanted to be God and not be human. They rejected life as the Creator offered it. The point of the story is that we all do this. Stories about our "first parents" are always about all of us. They wanted life without death, possibility without failure, potential without vulnerability, power without weakness. The problem is that real life includes all of these. To reject one side of the coin of life-as-it-is we reject being human. Because we want to safeguard our lives, we tend to gravitate to power to dominate others. Because we want to live, we tend to submit to those with more power than us. This happens on an almost pre-conscious level. From there, it begins to shape our perspectives, attitudes, and actions.

Separating these essential parts of life as it is, we get trapped in two possibilities:

- dominating others
- submitting to others

Once here, once we are separated from our own human goodness, we begin to create a society of domination and submission. We develop systems and policies to advantage some and take from others. We then claim that "this is just the way it is."

In our culture, which is so focused on the individual, we must realize that sin is not just an individual problem. It is expressed in our individual lives and in our collective lives. As Lutheran ethicist Cynthia Moe-Lobeda writes:

> The vital points are two: (1) Social systems or structures are created by people over time. What is constructed by human decisions and actions is subject to human agency. That is, it can be changed or dismantled by other decisions and actions. (2) Dismantling systemic oppression or systemic evil requires recognizing it as systemic, rather than merely a function of individuals. These may be two of this book's most important points.[48]
> Cynthia Moe-Lobeda

Jesus understood that the issue of sin was both systemic and at the heart of each person. His stump speech about the Kindom of God shows that it is both about each of us and about how we create systems of domination or mutuality. That is why Jesus spoke of the Kindom of God replacing the Kindom of Rome.

As a society trends more toward domination, we often act out in pain. We often seek pleasure that harms us and others and the creation. We then use the word "sins" in plural to describe our behaviors and attitudes when we are captivated by domination and submission. These sins harm both us and the earth.

> To set the mind on the flesh is death, but to set the
> mind on the Spirit is life and peace.
> Romans 8:6

Flesh, again, is a poetic word for the domination and submission culture of the Roman Empire–for the system it created. Trapped by this collective and system sin, without true appreciation for the gift of life, we can easily become focused on unhealthy and hurtful behaviors. As societies, we can become so trapped in the flesh of domination that we enslave people, engage in genocide, steal land, and replace true enjoyment with consumption.

But we don't have to live like that.

Good and Very Good

I have been with hundreds of people through the process of dying. I have found that those who, by the gift of the Creator, practiced embracing life-as-it-is are able to accept their immanent death much easier than those who did not. Three days before my Father died he said, "It has been a hard life, but a good life. I am grateful." Weeks before my mother died we asked her about her funeral wishes. She sat up, and for a brief time, and was as clear eyed as she ever was.

But once we have, at a very deep level, separated ourselves from the fullness of life, how do we become integrated again?

In the creation stories, God creates the earth and says, "Behold, it is good, very good." But humans can reject the goodness of our mortal existence because we would rather not die. We decide we want to be God and not human. The power of the Incarnation of Jesus is that God became a human and embraced human life-as-it-is.

When Jesus calls disciples to take up our cross daily, he is inviting us to embrace both sides of the coin, to embrace life-as-it-is. Martin Luther taught that when God speaks to us, God speaks to us in what he called "law and Gospel." God speaks in warning to our dominating and submitting self. God speaks good news that our life-as-it-is, our whole self, is loved. God's message to us works to reunite us to the full range of human life. Mary Lowe, a Lutheran theologian, has offered some updated language that I find interesting. She writes that when God speaks to us, God both **humbles and empowers us.**[49] God's messages that humble and empower work in concert to reintegrate us to embrace life as it is. We are both limited and mortal and full of potential and life–the good news is that our lives, as they are, have intrinsic worth.

This reintegration is hard work. It is also the heart of the spirituality of Baptism: daily death and resurrection. When I was young, I asked what this meant and was told that it meant to let the bad parts of our behavior die (as envisioned by my church and community). It was basically seen as a practice to make me more observant of my culture. For others, baptism was the insurance certificate that ensured a comfortable afterlife.

Baptism brings us to daily awareness and acceptance of life as it is. Luther said as much: "To be born anew, one must consequently first die and then be raised up with the Son of Man. To die, I say, means to feel death at hand."[50] To feel death close at hand leads to a new life.

Jesus' invitation to take up the cross leads us to baptismal awareness: that conscious and heartfelt grief for the reality of death and vulnerability is a necessary part of a vibrant, grateful life. God values us and loves us in our life as it is.

Humans tend to create domination cultures when we reject the human condition. We create cultures that propose that to be human is to be powerful, especially over other people. We do this not only as individuals but as in-groups. We assume that we only have two options: dominate or be dominated.

Jesus embraced his own humanity. He embraces ours and leads us to embrace life as it is.

Every day, Jesus embraced with courage the life that includes vulnerability. Every day, he died on a cross. Every day, he found affirmation from God beyond our idea of God. When he was arrested and sentenced to death on the cross, he felt all the things that any of us would have felt. But because he had learned to face the reality of death each day, he was able to move through those feelings and ask God to forgive those who did not know what they were doing.

Third Option

Being human was good enough for Jesus. In fact, life is good and very good.

Jesus offers a third option of mutuality. Some Definitions:

- Domination: We can deny death and limitation by saying that we are most fully human when we have power over others.
- Submission: We can postpone death by joining with other powerful people, even when it means we can't fulfill our own calling and respect our own beauty.
- Mutuality: We can learn to accept our limitation and mortality along with our power and life and live in mutual relationship with others, holding our inherent value in balance with others and all of life.

Yea, Verily, mutuality is the very core insight of the Three Abrahamic Teachings. Each of them holds the value of each person, each in-group, and the whole creation as valuable, inherently good, and worthy of love. Mutuality is the character of our relationships in the Kindom of God.

To be clear, Embracing life as it is doesn't mean we don't engage in harmful behaviors and attitudes. It just means we may be more open to recognizing and working to change.

Let's consider greed as an example. Greed arises from this fundamental rejection of life as it is. Out of fear of our vulnerability, we gather more wealth, often at the expense of other people, the planet, and future generations. Those of us entrapped by greed continually focus on acquiring more and more. When we buy a boat, we long for the bigger boat. It does not satisfy because human vulnerability remains. The bigger boat only provides relief for a moment. It is good for us to have our daily bread, but we don't live by bread alone.

Greed takes our whole life, all our time and, energy and desire, and leaves us with nothing.

Meaning, community, with gratitude for life are the only lasting and durable responses to our lives as mortal beings. These grow from our embrace of life as it is, as we have been embraced by our Creator.

The idea of sin I learned as a child, the cow pie theology I heard, was itself an expression of sin. Its message was not to warn us of rejecting the good and very good creation and Jesus' embrace of life-as-it-is. This cow pie theology teaches us that life should be rejected because human beings and the rest of creation are manure. This understanding of sin rejects "both sides of the coin of life" and invites us to do the same. It traps us in domination and submission. It says that we can't do better, so we don't need to try.

But the teaching of our tradition about sin can offer a third option, even if it has rarely done so. This teaching informs us of our capacity to reject life and life with each other.

We will still fall short of embracing our lives. I find myself in nearly every moment tempted to reject life as it is, and in every moment, I am embraced by my Creator. Salvation includes, amid our anxiety about life, being accepted by the God beyond our idea of God who calls us to embrace life-as-it-is and participate in God's reign of mutuality, the Kindom of God.

This understanding of sin shapes how we might talk of salvation. Remember that "salvation" means healing and wholeness for each and all and the earth.

Salvation comes from the Creator, who embraces us as a part of a good creation. Salvation is:

- the Creator's embrace of our lives
- beginning every day to embrace our own life-as-it-is
- beginning every day to honor the humanity, dignity, and worth of all
- beginning every day to steward the ecosystem for our fellow creatures and future life on the planet

This begins now amid our own culture trending toward domination. God is working with us to change the policies and practices that divide and destroy us. God is working to bring us and all creation to healing and wholeness, to a new heaven and a new earth.

My friend and Upper Skagit elder Kay Knott said to me: "The Creator makes each of us good, with important work to do for and with each other. She invites us to recognize our own worth and goodness. She invites us to recognize when we fall short. But She continues to love us into being."

Sin is not a shorthand word for saying we are bad. It is a shorthand word for how we can fail to accept our goodness, the goodness of others, and the creation. Sin is a useful concept and a deep and challenging critique of the human experience. It can help us to understand ourselves and our society. Such understanding can help us to create more possibilities.

But sin is not God. It is not the immovable rock that the Creator cannot move. Too often, Christians orient their lives around their conception of sin rather than the Creator's power to heal it. God is committed to healing and creating the world. For Christians, this is revealed in Jesus, in whom God fully embraced life as it is and fully embraces us. Jesus leads us to honor, embrace, and enjoy life as it is and hold all of life in God-given inherent worth.

If I were sitting at a table with Red and Dr. Hall, I would now answer a little more clearly.

The message of the Scriptures and the Creeds is, "Being human is so good that God joined us in being human." This reveals that we no longer must compete for goodness and inherent dignity. That gift is given in Creation and given in Jesus, and again in every breath, every heartbeat. We no longer must compete in a cycle of dominance and submission. Rather, because of the Creator's embrace, we begin, in mutual love, respect, honor, and enjoyment, to work with each other for the common good. We are no longer doomed to compete with other cultures and wisdom traditions. We are no longer trapped in exclusive in-grouping, dehumanization, and violence. We are all on the same team: Team Human—and really, more broadly, Team Earth or Team-All-of-Creation.

Section Four Bible Studies

Jesus Honoring Our Common Humanity

Matthew 25:31-46

'When the Son of Man comes in his glory, and all the angels with him, then he will sit on the throne of his glory. All the nations will be gathered before him, and he will separate people one from another as a shepherd separates the sheep from the goats, and he will put the sheep at his right hand and the goats at the left. Then the king will say to those at his right hand, "Come, you that are blessed by my Father, inherit the kingdom prepared for you from the foundation of the world; for I was hungry and you gave me food, I was thirsty and you gave me something to drink, I was a stranger and you welcomed me, I was naked and you gave me clothing, I was sick and you took care of me, I was in prison and you visited me." Then the righteous will answer him, "Lord, when was it that we saw you hungry and gave you food, or thirsty and gave you something to drink? And when was it that we saw you a stranger and welcomed you, or naked and gave you clothing? And when was it that we saw you sick or in prison and visited you?" And the king will answer them, "Truly I tell you, just as you did it to one of the least of these who are members of my family, you did it to me." Then he will say to those at his left hand, "You that are accursed, depart from me into the eternal fire prepared for the devil and his angels; for I was hungry and you gave me no food, I was thirsty and you gave me nothing to drink, I was a stranger and you did not welcome me, naked and you did not give me clothing, sick and in prison and you did not visit me." Then they also will answer, "Lord, when was it that we saw you hungry or thirsty or a stranger or naked or sick or in prison, and did not take care of you?" Then he will answer them, "Truly I tell you, just as you did not do it to one of the least of these, you did not do it to me." And these will go away into eternal punishment, but the righteous into eternal life.'

Reflection

The Son of Man is a figure from Daniel chapter seven. The Son of Man is the truly human one who comes to set the world to right. But the Son of Man rules with people, not over them.

Last judgment stories are a way to boil down the key values of God. They tell us what is important to the Creator. Simply put, it is recognizing and honoring human beings. When one of us is vulnerable, the rest of us are blessed by God to care for the other. The most vulnerable are those whom God identifies with. This is in stark contrast to the caste system of the Roman Empire, in which God is associated with those with the highest status.

In this parable, Jesus makes no theological, cultural, or traditional test. What the Creator values is how we value each other, especially when we are vulnerable. This is because the Creator values us. I will cover the words "eternal punishment" in a later chapter.

The Kindom of God is the community that values each person and the earth as God does.

Hey, What About This Verse?

Hebrews 9:22

Indeed, under the law almost everything is purified with blood, and without the shedding of blood there is no forgiveness of sins.

Reflection

This verse is often used as definitive proof that God 1) requires sacrifice through the shedding of blood to forgive, and 2) that Jesus is the only sacrifice acceptable to God, and 3) only those who receive forgiveness explicitly through Jesus can be forgiven–in other words, God can only forgive faithful Christians.

After the Roman Empire destroyed the Temple, animal sacrifice was no longer possible. Rabbis tell us that they transitioned from animal sacrifice as a primary spiritual practice to prayer, praise, and a life of love of neighbor as the sacrifice God desires (Hosea 6:6). In Hebrews, the author is working to help Jewish Christians make a very similar move.

It is true that some parts of the Jewish tradition focused on the importance and meaning of animal sacrifice. Hebrews references one of these traditions with this verse in part to honor the grief that Jewish people and Jewish Christians were experiencing at the loss of the Temple in 70 BCE. Then, the author lifts up the traditional, broader view that sacrifice is one of many spiritual practices that draw people closer to God and to each other (Eberhart and Schweitzer, p. 6).

> Thus, it was necessary for the sketches of the
> heavenly things to be purified with these rites. Still,
> the heavenly things themselves need better sacrifices
> than these.
> Hebrews 9.23

Hebrews honors the importance of sacrifice in the tradition. Hebrews quotes this verse but goes to say that sacrifice is not required to make God capable of forgiveness. To put it in Christian terms, sacrifice was a sacramental act. Sacraments offer humans a way to experience God's love and forgiveness. Through them, God empowers us for lives of meaningful service. But God's love is not dependent on sacraments. Rather, we experience God's love in, through, and with them. A parent may express love through a hug, but the love is not limited to that hug.

The writer is proposing that people don't need to offer animal sacrifice because God has drawn near to human beings in Jesus' risking himself for the benefit of human beings.

Those that use this one verse as "proof" that Christianity is a divinely established exclusive in-group seem to not read the rest of the text. Nor do they seem to read the many other verses about sacrifice in the Hebrew Scriptures. This way-too-simple interpretation of a complicated book also seems to ignore the context and intent of the text: to help Jewish Christians find ways to faithfully practice their faith after the grievous loss of the temple. Where they once experienced at-one-ment with God in animal sacrifice, they can faithfully experience this in the spiritual practices of the Christian tradition.

Our Jewish neighbors did something similar, as Rabbi Wiener suggested in this section.

Section Five: The Slander Machine and a Human Strategy

Key Question: What is our tradition's basic understanding of how to create the world we long for?

Summary: Every time human communication has changed, human societies have experienced challenges. Understanding the role and impact of social media is vital to creating a strategy to increase unity among the human family. I offer an overview of how social media has impacted us, a review of a human strategy to help re-member us to each other, and thoughts on how we can make a difference. This chapter will explore further the core Abrahamic belief that our theologies do not define God.

Chapter Twenty-One: Slander and Dehumanization

> Of three things my heart is frightened, and of a
> fourth I am in great fear: Slander in the city, the
> gathering of a mob, and false accusation—all these
> are worse than death.
> Ecclesiastes 26:5

In August of 2017, terrified Rohingya left their homes in Myanmar for Bangladesh. Over one million Rohingya are now living in a refugee camp in Bangladesh, and hundreds of thousands are in Thailand, India, Indonesia, and Nepal. In the beginning, there were tensions between the Buddhist majority and the Muslim Rohingya. Then, the slander ramped up. Rumors began to spread on social media that the Rohingya were going to attack their Buddhist neighbors. A Buddhist leader, widely condemned by other Buddhist teachers and leaders[51], began to refer to the Rohingya as rabid dogs that must be put down to protect the community. This led to genocide of the Rohingya.[52]

Of course, one of the key Buddhist teachings is not to engage in slander:

> To undertake the training to refrain from false
> speech. As well as avoiding lying and deceiving, this
> precept covers slander as well as speech which is not
> beneficial to the welfare of others.
> Precept 4[53]

In the 20th Century, over two-hundred-and-sixty million people were killed in genocide. People of all religions participated. People who denied religion participated. Germany in the 1930s had one of the most highly educated populations in the world. As in Myanmar, the wisdom tradition of the nation had been corrupted to promote exclusive in-grouping and dehumanization that led to violence. Hitler didn't have social media, but he did have a new communication tool: radio. He used it to spread slander against Jewish, Roma, disabled, and LGBTQIA+ Europeans.

As Ecclesiastes suggested, slander can lead to a mob, and a false accusation can lead to death.

Two-hundred-and-sixty million people is a lot of people. It takes many more people to participate in their murder, to bury bodies, to look the other way, to deny that it is happening.

We often imagine that genocide or violence against a group is carried out by people intending to do evil. With sadness, I report that this is not usually the case. What I have learned about the power of dehumanization is this: People participate in genocide and other forms of out-group violence because they are convinced it is morally right to do so. Dehumanization is often built on historical racism. Leaders use historic bias and bigotry as a foundation for dehumanization today. I present the process of dehumanization as a series of steps, but these steps often take place at the same time.

One: An influential person or group of leaders proposes an "Us vs. Them," an in-group versus an out-group. Often, they build on existing bias and bigotry. Muzafer Sherif showed that all that humans need to create tension is to propose two groups. This is powerful by itself. The power of such group division depends on who the leader is and how the leader communicates.

Two: They promote dehumanizing language about the out-group. They compare the out-group to animals and insects. They talk about how rapidly they procreate. They say the out-group is bringing disease. The larger community begins to use this language. People start to distance themselves from the out-group.

Three: Leaders begin to apply collective blame to the whole out-group for the behavior of some. These leaders say that "all of them intend to behave the same way." People begin to engage in violence against the out-group and call it retaliation.

Four: The leaders ramp up a sense of threat to the in-group, the majority wisdom tradition (for example, saying Christmas is under attack), and say that the out-group is part of a conspiracy to destroy the nation and harm the vulnerable. The fear becomes real, even if the threats are made up. Violence continues to increase toward the out-group.

Five: Leaders say there is a solution to this problem. They say that we have no choice. We must "get rid" of this dangerous out-group. It may be unpleasant, they say. We good people normally would not do this kind of thing, but we must protect all that is good and right.

Six: More people in the in-group begin to believe that violence is necessary and even morally good. They say, "We have to do this to protect women and children." The leaders say that "God is on our side" against this god-less horde who is forcing us to act this way. "A peaceful future awaits us if we act now."

In many conversations, presentations, reading, and hours of contemplation on dehumanization, I began to realize a terrible truth: Dehumanization works by targeting what we love, what we value, and what we hold most dear.

A man who cared for three daughters and was loving to his wife while she died of Alzheimer's was so angry with me for supporting Muslims that he could hardly speak to me. Why? He had heard terrible things about Muslims from politicians, news sources, and hate groups disguised as freedom-loving, apple-pie-eating patriots. They targeted what he loved and valued: women's rights. They did this in order to turn him against a religion that offered a set of women's rights unequaled in much of the world all the way back in the 6th century.[54]

My understanding of dehumanization borrows heavily from the work of Jonathan Leader Maynard who studies how the process of dehumanization works in mass killing.[55] Our love for our in-group, a good thing, is twisted to become the motivation for evil. The commandment, "Thou shalt not bear false witness against your neighbor," is wisdom's warning: We are all vulnerable to lies about the danger someone poses to our community. Our very desire for a safe community can be twisted to become the motivation for violence.

Hacking Human Nature

Human beings have always been vulnerable to this. However, the advent of social media has mechanized slander, and it has turbo-charged exclusive in-grouping and dehumanization. Max Fisher, in *The Chaos Machine*, charts the destructive power of social media. In 2015, Facebook produced an AI (artificial intelligence) to manage posts and interactions on Facebook with one goal:

Engagement. The more time people spend on social media, the more ads they see the more money social media companies get. The AI was set free to write the code that determined what we see in our social media feeds.

And what brings greater engagement? Activating and amplifying in-group/out-group tensions with **moral outrage**. Social media posts that propose an "Us and Them" with examples of the out-group transgressing moral norms regularly get the most engagement. So, the AI promotes posts with moral outrage directed toward out-groups and we see more of these posts. Then, our friends liked more of these posts. We begin to think it must be true because our friends have liked it. We begin to think it must be true because so many people seem to believe it.

> (Sean Parker, Facebook's first President) termed
> this the "social-validation feedback loop," calling it
> "exactly the kind of thing that a hacker like myself
> would come up with, because you're exploiting
> a vulnerability in human psychology." He and
> Zuckerberg "understood this" from the beginning,
> he said, and "we did it anyway." [56]
> Max Fisher

Let's go back to the quote from Ecclesiastes. Slander isn't lying about what color your neighbor likes or their sports team. Who cares? Slander is lying about how a neighbor is breaking the rules and endangering the community. The motivation that slander activates is love for the community. If people don't adhere to the norms that make the in-group function, then the whole in-group feels threatened. This threat drives violence. Social media amplified this from a person-to-person slander to machine-propagated poison.

> Certain social stimuli can, under the right
> circumstances, change our underlying nature. The
> conclusions, derived from newly available data,
> were bracing: online norms of ever-escalating
> outrage and conflict could "transform ancient social
> emotions from a force for collective good into a tool
> for collective self-destruction."
> Max Fisher quoting Molly Crocket

Social media created a slander machine that contributed to many of the violent episodes in our memory, including those in Myanmar, Sri Lanka; Christ Church, New Zealand; Charlottesville, VA; and Pittsburgh, PA. But Fisher argues that it is not some small piece of programming that is to blame. The whole design of these platforms is to create engagement through moral outrage, leading to exclusive in-grouping and dehumanization. Research has shown that when the Internet or Facebook was offline, intergroup violence decreased.

In 2021, Frances Haugen, a Facebook employee, brought forth internal research that showed that the negative impact of social media was both known and ignored.

> Facebook's executives, including Zuckerberg, had been plainly told that their company posed tremendous dangers, and those executives had intervened over and over to keep their platforms spinning at full speed anyway.
> Max Fisher

YouTube, Twitter, and other platforms are equally problematic. YouTube, says Fisher, is even worse. Just select a topic, watch a few videos, and watch how YouTube begins to tailor your suggested videos. Select a hot-button topic and see what happens–but beware: you may "go down the rabbit hole." The rabbit hole is a term from *Alice in Wonderland* used to describe how people get radicalized on social media platforms. These platforms lead many users to ever more radical sites, podcasts, and communities. The "Unite the Right" rally in Charlottesville, VA, only happened, Fisher writes, because isolated hate groups got connected by Facebook's AI. Now, all the extreme folks were becoming part of one larger extremist movement.

> The... A.I.'s had all independently arrived at some common, terrible truth about human nature. "I called it radicalization via the recommendation engine," Renée DiResta said. "By having engagement-driven metrics, you created a world in which rage-filled content would become the norm.
> Max Fisher

We have been witnessing and changed by a profit-driven, AI-powered, universally accessible slander machine gathered mobs with false accusations. At its worst, this has led to the murder of innocent people. It has also divided families, communities of wisdom, and neighbors. It has radicalized people, using what they love to manipulate them into hating and doing violence to their neighbors.

Recent studies have shown that the rabbit-holing process of YouTube has slowed. Alphabet has changed the programming behind what videos are suggested. It is unclear if other platforms are doing better. But all the social media platforms have already gathered together many individuals and organizations to strengthen hate groups in the United States.

Hate Groups

While this was visible in the Unite the Right rally in Charlottesville, VA, it continues today. Hate groups are actively recruiting people with their White Nationalist narrative. These people are finding meaning and community among those dedicated to the caste system, seeking to maintain it with violence and anti-democratic political leadership. It takes great effort and courage for them to escape this poisonous community. There are several things that contribute to this.

- Loss of connection to friends and family
- Hate groups have become their primary community
- Response to social pressure within their primary community

In his book *Ordinary Men,* Christopher Browning writes about Reserve Police Battalion 101. The battalion was comprised of middle-aged German professional men who were considered too old to go to the front during WWII. They were called together, trained, and sent into villages to round up and kill Jewish residents in occupied Poland. They were not told their specific mission until after they were deployed. Their commanding officer wept as he informed his men of their orders to kill an entire village of Jewish people—men, women, and children. He allowed them to opt-out if they objected to the assignment. Browning's research states that 80 to 90 percent of them did not opt-out. His explanation of why is chilling:

> Because it was easier for them to shoot. Why?
> First of all, by breaking ranks, non-shooters were
> leaving the 'dirty work' to their comrades. . .. It was
> in effect an asocial act vis-à-vis one's comrades.
> Those who did not shoot risked isolation, rejection,
> and ostracism—a very uncomfortable prospect
> within the framework of a tight-knit unit stationed
> abroad.[57]
> Christopher Browning

The social pressures that led Police Battalion 101 members to engage in horrific acts of violence are at work among members of hate groups.

Wisdom communities must play a greater role in preventing people from becoming a part of hate groups. We must step forward in public partnerships to show people that we can build a future together. We must strengthen the bonds of trust and relationship, offering hope for a better future together.

We Have Power

Haugen has said in many interviews that we must change the AI and computer programming to eliminate engagement-based, profit-driven social media. There could still be a social media, but it would have to be rebuilt.

> "I think we don't want computers deciding what
> we focus on," she said. She also suggested that if
> Congress curtailed liability protections, making the
> companies legally responsible for the consequences
> of anything their systems promoted, "they would
> get rid of engagement-based ranking."
> Max Fisher

But even if this happened, we would still be living with the united and emboldened extremists in our nation and around the world and family members susceptible to their slander.

I have spoken to hundreds of faith leaders about what is happening to humanity. Most all of them say, "Things are falling apart." Many also know that, for many groups, the world was never that "together," with the pervasiveness of racism, misogyny, and other forms of injustice. But these leaders agree: divisiveness is accelerating.

What can we do?

We have a choice. We can continue down this road of exclusive in-grouping, dehumanization, and violence. Or we can choose to do our part to bring our communities together to form a more perfect union, to recognize our common humanity. We will either stand together, or we will fall apart.

Social media companies have hacked human nature to bring out our worst. Those seeking to divide us have leveraged social media to terrible effect. It is likely that artificial intelligence will make this worse, as it is used to create images, videos, and messages to confuse us about what is real and what is not. AI will likely flood the zone with so much fear-inducing nonsense that many of us will withdraw.

But human beings have positive potential as well as vulnerabilities. We need to hack human nature to bring out these positive potentialities. Or, more clearly, we need wisdom that strengthens the things that can bring human beings together and help us to stay together while we work for the world we long for.

I believe that ancient traditions carry wisdoms to help us do just that. Let's Go Together grows from that wisdom. Let's turn to that next.

Chapter Twenty-Two: Human Strategy

> You have heard that it was said, "You shall love your
> neighbor and hate your enemy." But I say to you,
> love your enemies and pray for those who persecute
> you, so that you may be children of your Father in
> heaven; for he makes his sun rise on the evil and on
> the good, and sends rain on the righteous and on
> the unrighteous. For if you love those who love you,
> what reward do you have? Do not even the tax-
> collectors do the same? And if you greet only your
> brothers and sisters, what more are you doing than
> others? Do not even the Gentiles do the same? Be
> perfect, therefore, as your heavenly Father is perfect.
> Matthew 5:43-48

What do we do when social cohesion has been lost? What do we do when people feel a loss of trust, when people feel like everyone is an enemy? We need a human strategy. We need to understand both the positive potential of human nature and our common vulnerabilities. We need to learn how our positive potential can be strengthened, and our vulnerabilities lessened.

Jesus offers a human strategy in this passage.

Remember that the Roman occupation was a crisis of community, dividing people from each other. Under the conditions of scarcity and pressure by Roman soldiers, people had lost trust in each other. Remember that when John the Baptizer was asked what people could do, he focused on sharing food and clothing; he focused on activities to support each other's well-being.

Jesus is not being naïve; he understands what can invite human beings to come together and what can keep us divided.

Jesus doesn't say to get together with our enemies and debate politics, economic theory, or policy. His human strategy was to do good for each other, with each other, and to offer respect to each other in public. When we see each other as human, when we see each other as increasing our common well-being, and when we see groups respecting each other in public, our trust begins to grow. We start the process of removing fear from our hearts. We begin to laugh not at each other but with each other.

We begin to find our compassion, courage, and curiosity about each other.

Common Wisdom

I asked Genjo Marinello, a Zen Buddhist Priest, what his tradition says when social cohesion is lost. He said: "First, we need to look in each other's eyes, listen, and see each other as humans. Second, we need to come to some understanding of our shared values. Third, we need to do something that benefits the community together."

I have asked Zoroastrians, Hindus, Jewish Rabbis, Muslim Imams, Christian pastors, Indigenous Elders, Atheists, and Humanists the same question. There are differences, but the deep wisdom is very similar. When we know each other as humans, work for our common good, and show public respect to each other, social cohesion begins to grow. We may have different traditions, communities, and identities, but together, we form a larger identity that supports and benefits from the differences.

Once divided, groups become "We the people" while remaining ourselves.

Our Muslim friends often quote this verse from the Holy Quran about how we engage with people who believe we are enemies:

> The good deed and the evil deed are not equal.
> Repel by that which is better; then behold, the one
> between whom and thee there is enmity shall be as if
> he were a loyal, protecting friend.[58]
> Holy Quran: 41:34

From the Hebrew Scriptures:

> If your enemy is hungry, give him bread to eat; if he
> is thirsty, give him water to drink.
> Proverbs 25:21

Those who are tearing us apart understand human nature. They know that, if we are divided into groups we will be vulnerable to distrusting each other. They know that dehumanizing language will promote fear and violence. They understand that social media companies want money and how they have hacked human nature for their own greed. All of this is powerful.

However, our wisdom traditions understand human nature better than the dividers. If I must make a bet between social media, podcasts, and divisive politicians on the one hand and local, widespread, face-to-face relationships, work for the common good, and publicly demonstrated mutual respect for the other, I will take the latter. Real-world relationships in our neighborhoods and towns are more powerful than social media.

This is why the Let's Go Together strategy is to gather as diverse a group of people as possible and do these three things each year:

- eat and share stories
- do a service project day or weekend
- hold a public solidarity event

This is a powerful, replicable, and sustainable human strategy to counter the exclusive in-grouping and dehumanization that is eroding our communities. Research shows that when people experience events like these, they share them (in real life, not on social media) with twenty others. Trust begins to spread by word of mouth, by the kindness of faces, and by the generosity of our hands.

Social media is powered by AI. It's everywhere, all the time.

Assets In Each Other

But we have assets, too. In every neighborhood, town, and city, we have communities of wisdom who know how to do potlucks, develop relationships of trust, do service projects, and respect each other in public. Communities of wisdom can see how we are falling apart and want to do something about it. Their leaders do, too. Three events per year won't take over the mission of communities of wisdom, but it will enhance it.

The social sciences call this contact theory: getting to know people and cultures helps reduce our sense of fear. It begins to create the conditions for respect and even love. But social sciences also tell us that contact with other cultures can go wrong. Contact theory only works when it is done intentionally with respect, mutuality, and a common purpose.

There is such a deep hunger in the public for communities of wisdom to bring the best wisdom they have, to create spaces for relationship building, and to work together for the common good. People are longing for leadership at the local level.

There is longing to embody our common leadership, our ability to partner, our ability to recognize the unity in diversity of the creation, and our call to bless all peoples. There is longing for the Kindom of God to emerge between all peoples. There is longing for a love willing to risk for the well-being of our whole community. There is longing for hope in a sea of despair. There is longing to be invited and included in the work.

Christian congregations can find new purpose in taking our part in this leadership held in common.

In this conversation, our Muslim and Jewish neighbors talk about knowing and working with each other:

> Sheik Jamal: Now, today, we know that to really foster peace in the world, we simply have to practice what is called "coming to know the other on a human level." That seems to be the best way to overcome polarization, whether it's religion or, politics, or culture. In the '60s, in the program called Challenge, Father Treacy, Rabbi Levine, and some others had the revolutionary idea that it is critical, if we really want genuine peace in our world today, we have to dialogue. We have to connect on a human level by really listening to the other.

> Rabbi Yohanna: I would just say skepticism, as part of Judaism, is asking questions. Judaism is not a religion of answers. If you're going to identify it as a religion in any way, the most important thing to know is it's not about answers; it's about questions. It's your tradition where we help to form good questions that lead us forward into a healthy future. By poking at our own tradition, asking why, and asking if things can be different and does the world have to be this way, we move ourselves towards tikkun olam, towards the complete healing of our world, which some Jews will call the messianic era. That there will be a time when all of humanity and nature lie down with each other in peace and that we're working towards

that goal of wholeness and completion and beauty and goodness being the pervading movements in this world.

So, we join with all other religious traditions and civilizations who seek a planet at peace, a humanity at peace, a place filled with justice and goodness and mercy and compassion, which goes all the way back to number one, in the image of God, because we will chant on Yom Kippur, on the High Holidays, God's divine characteristics, "el Rehoom ya na rehoon," a God who is compassionate and loving, " el rachum," a God who is long-suffering, God who's full of truth. We chant those, and then we take that into ourselves, and we do the work the rest of the year to make that real in our world.

Chapter Twenty-Three: Meaning and the Mysterious Supreme

We do not live by bread alone but by every word
that comes from the mouth of God.
Jesus Quoting Deuteronomy 8:3

Human beings have physical needs that must be met for us to survive: food, clean air, water, shelter, clothing, medical care, safety, etc.

But we do not live by these basic needs alone.

Human beings need community. Throughout history, people have needed human company and relationships to survive. Being a part of a group is so beneficial to human survival that we are often willing to sacrifice our time and even our lives to benefit our in-group. Throughout human history, people have needed human company to feel that life is worthwhile and enjoyable. It is not good when we are lonely.

Human beings need meaning. Perhaps the marker of when our ancestors became human is when we developed stories, practices, and a capacity for self-critique that helps us understand our place in the world and the value of our community. These stories and practices shape what we get up for in the morning, what we do during the day, and what gives us a sense of accomplishment before we sleep.

It is possible that humans first gathered around public storytelling and symbols and that we created larger societies to meet our hunger for shared meaning. Meeting this hunger was so important to us that we developed agriculture so that we could live closer to each other.[59]

To survive and thrive, humans must meet basic needs, build community, and find or create meaning. Threaten any one of these, and we respond with deep anxiety. Anxiety can lead to violence. Because our vulnerable lives are made possible by the combination of these factors, to threaten them means to encounter our vulnerability, even our mortality.

We can all see how a threat to our basic needs threatens us. We can all see how another community or in-group can be perceived as a threat. The tendency for us to be cautious of other in-groups and to think highly of our own is called in-group bias.

When we encounter people of another wisdom tradition, we can respond with distrust. The stories, practices, and deep truths of our own tradition offer meaning, order, and a sense of purpose to our days. Our own tradition is woven into our in-group and how we meet our basic needs. Emotionally, we see them as part of one thing.

All human beings have a vulnerability here. We can see other in-groups and their traditions as a threat to us, as a threat to our existence.

I remember the first time I went to a Mosque. I was nervous and disoriented. I didn't know what to expect. I felt the same when I went to a Jewish Temple, attended a Buddhist ceremony, and was present at an Indigenous funeral. But in each case, I was warmly welcomed, could find much to appreciate, and found myself ready to explore my own wisdom tradition with fresh eyes.

Growing up in the Lutheran Church, I heard messages about God's love for all people. I also heard messages that said Christians have the only way to God, that we are superior to others, and that God might want to love people but simply can't if they aren't Christian. I have heard the same from people in all Christian traditions.

What our wisdom tradition teaches about other in-groups and other traditions can really impact how we react to others. While humans may be hardwired to be cautious of other in-groups and traditions, the "software" of our own traditions means a lot. Our response to others arises from nature, nurture, and experience.

When our tradition teaches exclusive in-grouping, we say things like:

- there is only one way to truth
- our way is superior to other ways
- we are the only real humans

These claims lead us down a path to what I call **exclusive in-grouping**. It leads us to see other groups as less than fully human and to see our meaning systems in competition. It leads us to see other groups as having less worth, dignity, and status. It leads to conflict. This is mono-religionism.

In my experience, most claims to interpret the Bible literally are a claim to power over other people. They are usually claims to exclusive in-grouping.

When our tradition teaches authentic, pluralist in-grouping, we say things like:

- there is only one Truth to which we aspire
- our way is one of many on the path to truth
- there are many expressions of true humanity

These claims lead us down a path of partnership with and respect for people of all wisdom traditions. We could call this **authentic, pluralist in-grouping**: it's good to be part of an in-group while recognizing the dignity and honor of other groups and traditions. These claims lead us to recognize a larger goal, a larger truth, and a larger path we can walk on with others.

Some key questions in this book are:

- Is exclusive in-grouping or authentic, pluralist in-grouping more faithful to the tradition of Jesus and the larger Abrahamic tradition?
- Which of these have Christians embodied through the centuries?
- What changes, if any, do we need to make to be more faithful to the vision of Jesus?

The Only Only

I was teaching at a conference about how Christians could support the civil and religious liberty of Muslims. While on a panel with Muslims, a woman asked, "Are you saying that Christianity is not the only way to God?"

I responded: "My tradition teaches me that we don't find God. God finds us and finds us where we are. My tradition also teaches that God is committed to finding us–and humans live and have lived in many cultures. I am grateful that God has continued to find me through my tradition and community. That is God's gift to me. However, that does not give me the right to tell God how to find people. It is not what we think about God that is ultimate. Our tradition is not supreme. Only the Creator is."

Anytime that humans use words, ideas, symbols, art, poetry, or stories to claim to have God figured out, it is an **idol**. The Ten Commandments were written down when the People of Israel were enslaved in Babylon. While enslaved there, they reflected on a previous experience in Egypt. Leaders in both Egypt and Babylon *at that time* claimed that the gods created their culture–and authorized enslaving others. It is easy for a good tradition to be twisted to support an unjust system. It is easy for a good tradition to be twisted to claim superiority. Every tradition can be used to do just that. That is why the Hebrew tradition sought to prevent this through its first teachings.

> I am the Lord your God, who brought you out of the
> land of Egypt, out of the house of slavery; you shall
> have no other gods before me. You shall not make
> for yourself an idol, whether in the form of anything
> that is in heaven above, or that is on the earth
> beneath, or that is in the water under the earth.
> Exodus 20:2-4

An idol is not just a statue or image. Idolatry is claiming our way, our tradition, our culture, our society, or our economy is ultimate. Humans use idols to:

- justify unjust systems
- to claim change is wrong
- claim that we are better than others
- remain passive to our neighbor's need
- keep leaders and the wealthy in power

Embedded in the first two commandments is a claim that the Creator has the right take on unjust societies. The One who "brought you out of the land of Egypt, out of the house of slavery" retains the right to challenge and change societies, traditions, economies, and cultures when they fall short of God's vision for human beings. God remains the only Supreme. Our human ideas are not supreme, not ultimate. God is sacred. Our thoughts and words about God are not.

Then the second commandment is a command to humility when communicating about God by forbidding the creation of idols.

God remains the only Supreme and is a Mysterious Supreme.

In the Abrahamic traditions, we tend to understand that God has chosen to reveal Godself to individuals and the community. But revealing oneself means showing a part. Moses doesn't see God but "only" a bright cloud. Elijah hears a wind, an earthquake, and a still, small voice. The Apostle Paul wrote that we "see in a mirror dimly." Again, as Paul Tillich taught, "We worship the God beyond our idea of God."

For Christians, the character of God has been revealed in Jesus Christ. But God retains the right to be more than we understand and different from what we assume.

When we forget that our theology, stories, and practices are not supreme, we begin a dangerous journey to exclusive in-grouping, dehumanization of others, and violence.

To put it another way: Our tradition begins with God's right to question and challenge our cultures and traditions; and remembering that humans are forbidden to claim that our view of God is ultimate. In short:

- the Creator remains the only only
- our tradition includes a central teaching about the limits of our own wisdom tradition.

Christians engage in idolatry in the way I have defined it, when we claim to be a divinely established exclusive in-group.

Our Muslim friends often quote this verse from the Holy Quran:

> God, there is no God but God, the Living, the
> Self-Subsisting. Neither slumber overtakes God
> nor sleep. Unto God belongs whatsoever is in the
> heavens and earth. Who is there who may intercede
> with God save by God's leave? He knows that which
> is before them and that which is behind them. And
> they compass nothing of God's knowledge, save
> what God wills. His Pedestal embraces the heavens
> and the earth. Protecting them tires God not, and
> God is Exalted, the Magnificent. There is no coercion
> in religion.
> Holy Quran, 3:255-256

God is the Mysterious Supreme. And, as in the Second Commandment, we respect the Mysterious One by not using coercive ways to force others to believe as we do.

The diversity of cultures, traditions, and ways of living is not a problem to be overcome but a gift to be enjoyed. In meeting, listening, and working together for the common good, we see a little more of the Divine glimpse of the Mysterious Supreme.

Holy Envy

Krister Stendhal, a Bishop in Stockholm, had a problem. A Mormon temple was being planned for Stockholm, and many people were publicly opposing it. How should he respond? After much prayer and thought, he proposed three rules when we engage another tradition: When trying to understand another religion, you should ask the adherents of that religion and not its enemies.

- Don't compare your best to their worst.
- Leave room for holy envy.

In this time of mass media there is much for us to learn from this.

I have encountered people from many wisdom traditions and cultures. I have found much in them that led me to a holy envy: a desire to find in my own tradition what I found in another. As Episcopal Priest Barbara Brown Taylor writes:

> When the Jewish Sabbath came up in class, I wanted it. Why did Christians ever let it go? When we watched a film of the God-intoxicated Sufis spinning, I wanted that too. The best my tradition could offer me during worship was kneeling to pray and standing to sing. My spiritual covetousness extended to the inclusiveness of Hinduism, the nonviolence of Buddhism, the prayer life of Islam, and the sacred debate of Judaism. Of course, this list is simplistic, idealistic, overgeneralized, and full of my own projections. It tells you as much about what I find wanting in my own tradition as it does about what I find desirable in another. This gets to the heart of the problem: with plain old envy, my own tradition always comes up wanting.
> Barbara Brown Taylor, Holy Envy

God as the Mysterious Supreme, however, is not only about what we do not know or the limits of our tradition—even though we desperately need clarity about this core teaching. God as the Mysterious Supreme is also an invitation to look forward to what we will discover, what God may continue to reveal, and the friends we will learn with and from. Holy Envy recognizes that God is beyond our understanding and God's freedom to reveal Godself to people in different contexts. Holy envy is the appreciation for how the mystery of God has been shown to others, as well as to us.

Honoring the mystery of God also honors the mystery of our own selves, who we are, and who we are becoming. God accepts all parts of me. God is creating me. God is creating us as in-groups and traditions and as one human family.

Chapter Twenty-Four: Your Why
and Effective Messaging

I grew up in a town of 300 people. I know what happens when we start hanging out with "the wrong people."

As you and your community of wisdom begin to relate to people of diverse cultures and traditions, someone is going to ask you a question: Why are you hanging out with them? You may be asked this by people in your community of wisdom, your family, friends, coworkers, folks at the golf club, or quilting group. Your response will depend on what you hold in common with them.

I have been asked "Why?" many times.

Here is my response: "Because of Jesus."

This does not need to be your response. I have other responses, too, depending on who asks and how we relate:

- I was bullied as a kid, and I want to create a world with no bullying.
- I believe in liberty and justice for all.
- Our society will not thrive unless we have equity for all people.
- I believe that God created all people in God's image.
- Jesus publicly related to diverse people.
- Because it's fun and we can share all our good food.

Each of these is more than a statement. Each one is a part of my deep "why" for working for unity, equity, and peace. They reflect a part of my deep values, my purpose in life, and my sense of what it means to be human.

Each of these statements can lead to a conversation, even a debate. You may or may not be ready for a long discussion or a debate. You don't have to debate. Ever. Unless you want to and have the time and energy.

Most of the time, a brief expression of your "why" will be enough. It will lead people to think more deeply about their own values and their own "why." Remember that most of the time, people change after our conversation is over. Let them reflect on your simply stated: "why." Trust people to be moved by the Creator. You don't need to change anyone.

Your "why" is powerful. Because it is yours, you cannot be wrong. People may disagree with you about it. But all you really have to say is, "I hear your point of view." Or "Thank you for teaching me about your point of view."

By clarifying our own "why" and listening to the "whys" of others, we learn a lot about ourselves. And it can be fun!

Challenges to Change

If you choose to engage in conversation with those gripped by fear, you will need to use all the wisdom you have. This book is an exploration of the challenges to change from exclusive in-grouping and dehumanization. I will summarize some key ideas here to help you gather your wisdom:

- **In-groups**: Human beings survived because we participated in in-groups. We instinctively tend to trust people in our in-group, and to distrust those who are not.
- **Desire of Life and Fear of Death:** Human beings are among the creatures on this planet that know we will die. We desire life but know we are vulnerable. This is just under the surface of our consciousness. When a threat is proposed, whether it is a reasonable threat or not, we can respond as if the threat is almost creating death itself. We want to get rid of it. If that threat is perceived as a group of people, then violence against that group can be justified– even when the threat is not real.
- **What We Love:** It is important to recognize that what we fear is mostly connected to defending what we love. Dehumanization is powered by the perception that what we love is being threatened by a whole group.
- **Instinctive Reasoning:** In his book *Righteous Mind*, Jonathan Haidt writes that most of the time, human beings make their decisions instinctively and unconsciously. We then use our rational minds to "backfill" our decisions with rationale. Once our choices are made, there are powerful

forces in us that keep us from changing

- **Confirmation Bias:** Once we have a point of view that we have acted on and justified, we then receive information that affirms that point of view, and we reject information that might lead us to question our point of view. Facts, data, and shaming communication often only cement people further in their view. It is important to remember that we all need to make choices to survive and thrive. It is unsettling to consider that if we are wrong about a bias, we may be prone to bad decisions that will harm us. Because humans tend to seek comfort, we tend to avoid thinking about things that are unsettling.
- **Associations:** Human beings see people more through what we associate them with than through facts or data.

Keys to Change

- **Influence Your In-group:** We are more likely to be open to someone in our in-group than others. We all have the most influence and responsibility to lead and model change in our own communities because that is where people are most likely to listen.
- **Positive Stories:** The best way to counter slander is positive, truthful stories. Jesus modeled this in his story of the Good Samaritan. He showed people that the Samaritans loved what they loved. Further, since human beings see people more through what we associate them with than with any facts or data, sharing positive stories about that group can create new associations for people.
- **Shared Values:** We all have values that are important to us. While we may differ on some values, we have many in common. When people see that you value what they value, their trust in you will grow, even if you differ on how to enact that value.
- **Work for the Common Good:** When people see group members, they fear working for the common good with members of other groups we trust; our fear is lessened. In other words, we must not just tell but help show the humanity of dehumanized groups.
- **Experiences:** We are shaped by our experiences. One powerful way to invite change is to share an experience with

someone captivated by fear, where they can see diverse people living life and doing normal things without having to engage them directly. Once they see they can have coffee in a gathering place of diverse people having fun, they will relax a bit. Offer people an experience like this and gently, carefully help them reflect on it.

- **Relationships:** When people hear a positive story, they change. When they have a relationship with a person in the group they have a bias toward, people really change. Invite the person to meet someone from the feared or hated group.

Communicating for Change

The following process for communicating for change was created in collaboration with the staff at the **Shoulder-to-Shoulder Campaign**. I am blessed to be in partnership with them. I encourage you to take their trainings for how to counter anti-Muslim bigotry. That training can help you counter bigotry toward other groups as well.

Meet the emotion, not the falsehood that leads to fear: Let the person know you hear how they are feeling, but do not repeat any falsehoods! This takes practice. We do not want to reinforce negative associations.

Reframe with a larger "we": Consider how you can take the person's concern and help to show that their concern is shared by all human beings, including the group that is feared.

Build on shared values: Listen deeply for values you share with your conversation partner. How can you affirm at least parts of what they value? Are you a part of an in-group with them? What values, stories, and practices can you build on to build trust in this conversation?

Tell a positive story: Share a positive story about the feared group. It is especially helpful to show the feared group working for the common good.

Follow up with some data: Share some data from studies about the feared group to show that the one positive story is actually representative of that group–more than negative stereotypes.

Frame a choice for our future: Find a way to share that our future is brighter when we stand together for safe communities, human rights, and opportunities for everyone

Invite them to walk a path with you: Ask when you think the timing is right for them to go and meet people from the feared group. Take it slow. Tell them how you once saw the feared group negatively and how you have changed over time.

Finally, be patient. None of us change because someone else makes us a project. Be true to yourself, be authentic and honest, and give them the time they need–realizing that they may not choose to change. Take breaks when you need to.

Messages that Work

As we listen to people, we can find common values that we share with them and that dehumanized groups share with them. There are many such messages contained in this book. Here are a few that I have found to work well.

- We believe in freedom of religion in this nation. All people have the right to pray or not pray as they choose.
- We believe that we, the people, can form a more perfect union together. We are stronger together.
- We don't want a country where people are endangered because of their identity. We want a nation where everyone is valued and honored as a part of We the People.
- We should learn about people directly from them, not about them from third parties.
- It is wrong to apply collective blame to a community for the acts of individuals.
- While Samaritans were from different racial and religious in-group, Jesus honored the humanity of Samaritans by accepting their hospitality.
- God's vision in the Abrahamic tradition is to bless all the nations of the world.
- The one Creator invites us to see the humanity of all people and cultures God has made.

I encourage you to use the questions in Discussion Questions, Action Steps, & Resources on our website to help you develop your "why."

Section Five Bible Studies

Jesus Honoring Our Common Humanity

Mark 7:24-30

From there Jesus set out and went away to the region of Tyre. He entered a house and did not want anyone to know he was there. Yet he could not escape notice, but a woman whose little daughter had an unclean spirit immediately heard about him, and she came and bowed down at his feet. Now the woman was a Gentile, of Syrophoenician origin. She begged him to cast the demon out of her daughter. He said to her, 'Let the children be fed first, for it is not fair to take the children's food and throw it to the dogs.' But she answered him, 'Sir, even the dogs under the table eat the children's crumbs.' Then he said to her, 'For saying that you may go—the demon has left your daughter.' So she went home, found the child lying on the bed, and the demon gone.

Reflection

Men and women did not speak in public if they were not related. As a person from another in-group, Jesus should have ignored her. He certainly should not have engaged in a public debate with her. But Jesus engaged with her and debated with her–in public.

Public debates in that century included very powerful language. Jesus challenged her with the comments about dogs. He compared her and her people with dogs–the equivalent of rats. And he debated with her in front of other people!

Her answer challenged him and the whole community to confront how they saw people of her culture–as being excluded from full humanity. She won the debate, and Jesus was not angry. He was not concerned about his status. He offered healing from the Creator for her daughter.

Hey, What About This Verse?

Acts 4:12

There is salvation in no one else, for there is no other name under heaven given among mortals by which we must be saved.

Reflection

This is another example of a verse often quoted to say that Christianity is the only way to God and God's only way to us. In this passage, Peter and the Apostles are very early in their ministry after Pentecost. Peter healed a paralyzed man in a public space, just as Jesus had. Word began to spread. Peter and John were arrested.

The key to this passage is what "salvation" means. Salvation means bringing wholeness, healing, peace, and justice to individuals and the whole community. Some churches seem to use salvation as a term referring to going to heaven when you die or being a recognized part of their exclusive in-group. It's important to consider who the "we" is in "by which we must be saved." Peter was speaking to the current situation of his own Jewish community under Roman occupation. Many Jews believed that a messiah would come and restore Israel to God's vision and would bring resurrection to those who had died under unjust rulers to experience life as it should be. Many groups in leadership among the Jewish people resisted the idea of a messiah because it stirred up revolution. The Chief Priests referenced this in their concerns about Peter's teaching. Peter was saying that Jesus is this longed-for messiah, even if he restored Israel to God's vision differently than people had expected. Instead of completing the work, Jesus invited people to continue this messianic work of healing and peace-making until his return. The Chief Priest, who was under much pressure from the Roman governor, could simply not afford to allow such a revolutionary movement to take hold. Otherwise, the governor would likely kill the Chief Priest, wage war on the Jewish people, and destroy the Temple.

Peter, fresh from his experience of the resurrected Jesus, was no longer as daunted by the terror of the Empire. He saw Jesus' resurrection from the dead as an invitation for all his community to shake off the shackles of fear, begin to love God and their neighbor and change the Empire from within. He stated his faith in Jesus as the one through whom God was providing this invitation to all of

Jesus' people.

Again, we often take verses meant for a specific situation and apply them everywhere. But God sent Jesus into this specific situation of imperial bondage. Understanding of Jesus' specific situation was lost for many centuries. This has led to almost uncountable, wild misunderstandings of Jesus' actions and words.

We see in Jesus the wholeness, healing, peace, and justice God intends for all people as expressed in his context. As it says in Isaiah

'It is too light a thing that you should be my servant
to raise up the tribes of Jacob
and to restore the survivors of Israel;
I will give you as a light to the nations,
that my salvation may reach to the end of the
earth.'
Isaiah 49:6

This means that the specific situation in which Jesus was bringing salvation also represents God's desire to bring healing to every context that falls short of God's vision. I have learned to respect the Creator's freedom to engage with other cultures in the way they need to be engaged. This does not lessen the importance of Jesus' mission and the beautiful tradition Jesus began.

Section Six: The Earth is Not the Titanic

Key Question: What is our tradition's understanding of hope for life on earth and humans as part of it?

Summary: At their best, wisdom traditions help us to find meaning, community, and hope for ourselves and the world. Some have told the Christian story in ways not fully faithful to Jesus, blessing unjust systems, and increasing despair. Yet, throughout our history, people have been called to a more faithful story. Some responded with courage in the face of injustice, and embodied hope in their time and place. In this section I will ponder hope for life on earth, another way to understand accountability to God in a moral universe, and how we find meaningful life working to bless all of life.

Chapter Twenty-Five: Blessing Despair

On April 10, 1912, the Titanic took off from England to New York on its maiden voyage. Brochures of the ship promoted it as unsinkable. A deckhand was quoted as saying, "Not even God himself could sink this ship."

This belief led the White Star Line to put only one-half of the necessary lifeboats on board and the captain to ignore warnings about large icebergs in the path to New York. They were so secure in their belief in the unsinkability of the Titanic that they took unnecessary risks and justified their careless behavior. On April 14, they hit an iceberg. The next day, the ship slid into the sea. Only 705 of the 2,200 passengers and crew survived.

We are familiar with this story because most of us have seen the movie *The Titanic*. When we watch this movie, we already know the ending. The only drama that remains for us is who will make it to the rescue boats and how well will the ship's quartet play.

Today, many people think life on Earth is like watching a movie about the Titanic. Some believe that the earth is the Titanic and that it will soon hit an iceberg and go down. Some believe, with the reverse arrogance of the deckhand, that not even God can save this ship–that is, not even God can save the earth. In either case, all we need to do is sit back, enjoy some good food and champagne, and make sure we have quick access to the lifeboats. We would only need to be concerned with our own and our family's survival and comfort. Any activity toward building up the earth in a sustainable way would be like re-arranging deck chairs on the Titanic.

These narratives deepen passivity and despair.

Our story about the ultimate future of the earth doesn't just describe the future. It tells us what to work for now.

Sadly, many Christians have bought into a false reading of Christian Scriptures. Jesus, they say, is coming soon to destroy a world near you. The earth is like a cheap rental house slated for destruction. Go ahead and punch a hole in the wall. Leaky faucet? Let it drip. This blesses passivity. It undermines the Three Great Teachings and empties love of its power.

Everything from the *Late, Great Planet Earth* to the *Left Behind* series casts the Biblical story as a narrative of despair and passivity. Our only hope, they say, is to get in good with Jesus so we'll have a spot on the lifeboat.

My uncle John was a Lutheran pastor. He came to visit us when I was in eighth grade. He believed that Jesus would come in 1983, at the High Holy Days of the Jewish people. My dad told him that I was a good student, a good citizen and that I was a capable basketball player. My dad said this to encourage me. My uncle told me, "Well, Terry, I am sorry to say it, but that won't matter because the world will be ending before you can go to college." I felt deflated and hopeless and was tempted to see my life and the life of the world as a worthless investment.

Further, these narratives tell us who we should love. They suggest that only Christians will be gathered to God. The rest will be rejected. These false interpretations encourage and enable Antisemitism in our own time. They suggest that the establishment of the State of Israel is a necessary step in the pre-planned destruction of Jews who do not convert to Christianity. When this is proposed as the ultimate fate of the Jewish people, it gives Divine blessing to violence against Jewish people now. These dehumanizing stories lead to violence against Jews, Muslims, and people of other faiths in the guise of "Biblical prophecy" and in the name of God.

In her book, *Rapture Exposed*, Lutheran pastor and professor Barbara Rossing shows how unbiblical this story really is. She says that the point of telling the story this way is to disempower us, to bless consumerism, and to make the way things seem inevitable and unchangeable.[60] This narrative of despair functions just like ancient stories that claimed that the gods created unjust systems. They say that God might not want the world to be this way, but there is nothing either God or you can do about it. So, take what you can, enjoy what you can get your bowl of popcorn, and wait for the world's destruction.

In this way, the earth as the Titanic empties our teachings of their meaning. What does stewardship of the earth mean in a world doomed to destruction? Nothing. What could love for neighbor mean when so many are doomed to destruction unless they think and believe and pray like us. Not much. In this narrative of despair, love is reduced to making other people Christian so that they can get on a lifeboat, too, and then the good people will get out of here.

Restoration of the Good and Very Good Creation

N. T. Wright, like Rossing and many others, rejects this "Earth is the Titanic" storyline.

> God's plan is not to abandon this world, the world
> which he said was "very good." Rather, he intends
> to remake it. And when he does, he will raise all
> his people to new bodily life to live in it. That is the
> promise of the Christian gospel.
> N. T. Wright

Biblical scholars and theologians are telling us that the message of the Scripture is not the destruction of the world but its healing. The word "salvation" means healing. Faithful lives don't prepare us to "get out of here" but, rather, to risk ourselves, as Jesus did, for the healing and creation of the world.

God created a good and very good creation and entrusted it to the stewardship of human beings.

> God blessed them, and God said to them, "Be
> fruitful and multiply, and fill the earth and subdue
> it; and have dominion over the fish of the sea and
> over the birds of the air and over every living thing
> that moves upon the earth."
> Genesis 1:28

Dominion here does not mean domination or exploitation. It means that human beings are in stewardship of the earth, its ecosystem, and all of life on this planet.

The Israelite tradition recognized that human beings fall short of this mark. The word "sin" in the Abrahamic tradition means missing the mark of the Three Great Teachings:

- love God more than our in-group and tradition
- love your neighbor as ourselves
- steward a thriving ecosystem and an equitable economy

There are several Greek words for "end." The main one used in the Christian Scriptures is *telos* which often means completion or goal. The "end of the world" most often in the Christian Scriptures does not mean the termination of the world, but rather the goal toward which God is at work in the world.

> And I saw a new heaven and a new earth: for the
> first heaven and the first earth were passed away;
> and there was no more sea.
> Revelation 21:1

The earth is neither unsinkable nor doomed. Its good and very good life is imperiled, and in Christ, God is calling Christians to care for it based on the deep values of the Abrahamic tradition. God is not calling us to wait for the world to end but to strive for the "end zone" or goal of the world, which is a healed, whole, and sustainable ecosystem

The World's End Zone

Our mission is not to gain access to the lifeboat on a doomed earth but to do all we can toward the healing of the ecosystem and to bring unity within the human family. Our small, often faltering efforts are then woven together into the tapestry of healing that God promises.

This does not mean that something isn't concluding or terminating.

> And as he sat upon the mount of Olives, the
> disciples came unto him privately, saying, "Tell us,
> when shall these things be? And what [shall be] the
> sign of your coming, and of the end of the world?"
> Matthew 24:3

The Greek word here is *suntelos,* which means conclusion or termination. What is concluding or being terminated is not the earth but the worldview of domination culture. First Century people used the word "world" much the same as we do:

- the earth and all of life
- the worldview, culture, or ways of human beings and society

In Matthew 24, Jesus is talking about the end of an age or worldview of destruction, bullying, scarcity, colonization, enslavement, and environmental degradation. This is good news! In Revelation, this is the fall of "Babylon the Great:" the symbol in Revelation for a culture taken over by domination. Until then, as

Jesus responds, we are called to witness to the goal of the healing and recreation of the earth until it comes in its fullness.

> Heaven is important, but it's not the end of the
> world.
> N. T. Wright

Healing the Nations

The Abrahamic tradition begins with God's primary value of blessing all the peoples, nations, tribes, cultures, and religions of the world. The Christian vision of the re-creation of the world honors this:

> The nations will walk by its light, and the kings
> of the earth will bring their glory into it. Its gates
> will never be shut by day—and there will be no
> night there. People will bring into it the glory and
> the honor of the nations. But nothing unclean will
> enter it, nor anyone who practices abomination or
> falsehood, but only those who are written in the
> Lamb's book of life. Then the angel showed me the
> river of the water of life, bright as crystal, flowing
> from the throne of God and of the Lamb through the
> middle of the street of the city. On either side of the
> river is the tree of life with its twelve kinds of fruit,
> producing its fruit each month; and the leaves of the
> tree are for the healing of the nations.
> Revelation 21:24-22:7

The end zone of the world is the healing and re-creation of the world and the reconciliation of all in-groups and traditions to one another. A time when exclusive in-grouping, dehumanization, and violence are no more. Domination itself, symbolized by Babylon the Great, is no more.

Living Toward Hope

Domination and its exclusive in-grouping, dehumanization, and violence will one day be ended, replaced by the Kindom of God. Between now and then, our role is to take part with God in the healing of the world.

God saves us not by snatching us out of the world,
but by coming into the world to be with us. This is
the central message of Jesus' incarnation and of the
Bible.
Barbara Rossing

Jesus' resurrection means that we can risk ourselves for the healing and creation of the world, we can live out love for ourselves and others, and God will have our back. Love wins. Life wins. The Kindom of God is on the way, and we get to live into it in the here and now. Christianity is a tradition in which we are invited to live in a vision of the world that will one day be fully realized. This vision is an Abrahamic vision: blessing all *mishpachah* in a world of kinship and mutual respect within a healed and whole earth.

My uncle was wrong about the Earth being destroyed in 1983. But his error, and all of those who fall for this narrative of despair, was deeper than that. He gave up on the good and very good creation of God and our collective responsibility to it and joy in being a part of it.

Like many Christians, Douglas John Hall taught me that the core of Christian teaching is this: God is committed to healing the earth. I have added this: God is committed to healing and creating the earth.

This is the basis of our commitment to ourselves, our diverse siblings, and the creation. This deepens the meaning of the Three Great Teachings upon which hang our ethical and moral reflection. What we do matters. The policies of our governments matter.

Our ecosystem and human community are facing extraordinary challenges. In the next century, we will go through challenges on an unprecedented scale. But the Earth is neither unsinkable nor doomed. Work on its behalf is not re-arranging deck chairs. Both the ecosystem and human community are worth risking for. Our mission is to do all we can to contribute to the vision of the Kindom of God in partnership with each other, trusting that God's Kindom will come on earth as it is in heaven. Grounded in a hope beyond what we can perceive, we live toward hope's fulfillment.

Chapter Twenty-Six: Singing a Deeper Song

When that woman stood over me in the narthex of the church and said, "If your family were better Christians, your mother would not be ill," it really hurt.

Thus, she ushered me into the arena of theology. It was a bullying thing to say. It was mean and mean-spirited. And it revealed her own fear of life and death and how she hoped she could avoid her own vulnerability by conforming to "Christian expectations." It revealed her own captivity.

It was a lie that held me captive for many years. It held her captive as well.

Some of what my church taught was not true to Jesus. Some of what they taught was damaging. They taught that God gave one religion and could only love you if you were part of it. They taught me that my Jewish neighbors were lost unless they accepted Jesus as we said we did. They taught me that God somehow needed violence toward and suffering of Jesus to be able to forgive us. They taught me that Jesus was coming to destroy the world, cast all unbelievers into hell and that I would be lucky not to be among them. They said no word about the Indigenous people whose land they farmed.

They also taught me things in the parking lot that were not true to Jesus. They taught me that it was okay to claim exclusive in-group status as white Christians. They taught me to use dehumanizing language against Jews, Mexicans, Black people, LGBTQIA+ people, and Indigenous peoples. They taught me that the well-being of these others was not my concern. They taught me that it might make right and that what really matters is making money and having high status.

You might ask, "Then why did you stay? Why did you become a pastor?"

Well, the pastor's wife hugged me every Sunday morning. The pastor preached from his heart a kind of love that his words did not fully convey. Ann Emerson explained what circumcision was to our fourth-grade class like a boss. People would ask how we were doing and show us kindness. They were generous to my family when times were hard. A member of the church gave my brother a loan to go to graduate school. They made Norwegian food like lefse and had potlucks with Jell-O "salads." They gave us kids bags of candy and peanuts for Christmas. The pastor used to ask me to read lessons, and even though I stuttered terribly, they listened in patience until I gained the confidence to speak in public. I would not be where I am without them.

I learned many good things from my family and from my church. Both have shaped who I am and what I do. They honored this reality by remembering, as Lutherans do, the Reformation and the need to continually be reforming the church. The very Jesus they taught me about could question and challenge what they taught me about Jesus.

My home church has also grown. They are not in the same theological and intellectual place they and many churches, social clubs, and the culture were in the 1970s and 80s. The Spirit of God continues to work in all of us.

That's why I stayed. They sang a song deeper than the lyrics and practiced a love beyond their theology. Perhaps we can only hope to do the same. Maybe we are all at our best, learning and growing. I trust the Creator to walk with us on that path.

This is not only my story. You, dear reader, also had a seven-year-old self. Perhaps you learned things in Sunday School and in the parking lot that you are recovering from. We are not alone. There are many who want to hear and sing that deeper song, express a love beyond mere words, and take part in the ongoing love of God.

A More Faithful Vision

Our organization, Paths to Understanding, was founded by Rabbi Rafael Levine and Father William Treacy. Rabbi Levine died in 1985. Father Treacy died in the fall of 2022. In the last six months of Father Treacy's life, I asked him to summarize what being human is all about. First, he said that "the role of wisdom traditions is to bring the love of God in the world to our awareness." Wisdom traditions don't create or control that love, but they can help us to experience it and be challenged to participate in it. Then he said:

> We are here to learn to love each other, ourselves,
> and all that the Creator has made because the
> Creator loves all of us.
> Father William Treacy

This reminds me of what my friend Jay Bowen has said: As a spirit goes to earth, the Creator says, "Enjoy yourself, help people, don't hurt anyone." Father Treacy and I would often talk about how Christianity had fallen short of Jesus. He didn't believe that God needed Jesus' suffering to be able to forgive. Rather, he believed that Jesus risked his life to show us the extent to which God will go to love human beings and the earth. Made in the image of God, we find our meaning in joining Jesus in this love.

We often talked about the healing and renewed creation that God promises. With sadness, we spoke of the doom-and-despair fiction that so many have made of the "end of the world."

We spoke of the role of Christian prayer and spiritual practices to prepare and sustain us for a life of love and meaning.

> Jesus was inviting a community so captivated by
> their own human dignity, and so committed to the
> dignity of others, that we would be willing to risk
> anything to honor that dignity.
> Father William Treacy

Until he died at one hundred and three years old, Father Treacy was working to recover a more faithful vision of Jesus. I hope to do the same.

So many others are doing the same kind of work to see the radically loving God that our tradition professes. Here are some quotes to show the kind of work people are doing.

> [God] is disclosed as the God of history, whose
> revelation is identical with his power to liberate the
> oppressed.
> James Cone, Black Theologian

> Creation is filled with the life-giving, life-saving, life-
> sustaining, and life-savoring power of a God whose
> love for this world cannot be thwarted by any force
> in heaven or on earth.
> Cynthia Moe-Lobeda, White Feminist Theologian

We must resist the dangerous temptation to tame
Jesus until he looks like the very empire that hung
him from a tree.
Lenny Duncan, Black Lutheran Pastor

The gospel that was twisted to accommodate
America's original sin [of racism] must also be
reconstructed if we are to experience the healing that
Jesus wants to bring.
Johnathan Wilson Hartgrove, White Southern
Theologian

The challenge for Lutheran [Christians] is to
embrace fully the ethics of freedom we claim to be
central to our theology and to live out the tenant of
this belief, allowing space in God's kingdom for all
of God's people.
Beverly Wallace, Black Womanist Theologian

I want [my granddaughters] to know the meaning
of new life in relation to that real pain caused by
sin, the new life of the resurrection. No pain from
sin, no need for the cross. No cross, no need for the
resurrection. But there is pain; we know there is.
There's sin that causes pain. There is God's love in
relationship with that pain through Jesus Christ. But
there is also resurrection.
Alicia Vargas, LatinX Womanist Theologian

[The message of the cross] is not to reveal that our
condition is one of darkness and death; it is to reveal
to us the One who meets us in our darkness and
death. It is a theology of the cross not because it
wants to put forth this ghastly spectacle as a final
statement…. but because it insists that God…meets,
loves, and redeems us precisely where we are: in the
valley of the shadow of death.
Douglas John Hall, White Canadian Theologian

All these folks, and thousands more, are working to go to the roots of our tradition, to be honest about how we have warped it, and to strive for a more faithful vision of Jesus and his Kindom.

You and I are not alone on this journey of recovery.

And there is something more.

In the Abrahamic tradition, we understand that the wind blows where it will. The Spirit's living breath continues to breathe new life into us because God wants to. God calls prophets to speak the hard truth, storytellers to help us imagine the new heaven and the new earth, and all of us to encourage one another as we walk the path together. God continues to re-imagine us, to help us connect to ourselves and each other, and to help us enjoy one another again.

I still have things to say to my seven-year-old self. He has things to say to me. I imagine that you may be having similar conversations with yourself. Some things are becoming clearer to me, including how we understand the idea of hell.

Chapter Twenty-Seven: Broken Doors, Open Gates

Father Treacy and I had many talks about the idea of heaven and hell. I only wish I could have talked with Rabbi Levine about that, too! We agreed that the Creator cares about how we treat each other and the earth. We agreed that God holds us accountable for how we fall short of love for ourselves and each other. We agreed that the God revealed in Jesus could not lovingly create sentient beings and then hand them over to torture for all eternity. We agreed that this idea turned a moral universe into a prison and distorted a God of steadfast love into a sadistic prison warden. The purpose of accountability is reconciliation, not eternal torture.

Few ideas in Christian belief strengthen exclusive in-grouping as much as the idea of hell. This will be a longer chapter because it's so complicated. For about a year, I decided not to write about it at all due to the powerful feelings this topic evokes. But I had some conversations that changed my mind. I hope this helps you as much as writing it helped me.

Refining Love

My Father was always very intentional about offering words of affirmation for me. Few days went by without him saying something supportive or encouraging. In seventh grade, I was not applying myself to my studies very well. I was getting B's and even some C's. My Dad asked me to sit in his chair. He was angry because I wasn't working very hard on my studies. He told me that he wanted better for me and that he wanted me to have options for work and life that only education could bring. He told me with tears that he wanted me to have more opportunities than he had. My Dad left school to work on the farm that would later be sold out from under him. He never graduated from high school and knew that limited his options. I can still feel the burning in my stomach and my skin as I encountered my Father's anger about my actions and inactions. It felt like hell. But his tears made it clear that his anger was an act of love. It was "for me," not against me. I was the one who was against me, and he wanted me to know it in time to change.

As we begin to consider the idea of "hell," consider my Father's anger. His anger grew from his love for me. Real anger is an expression of love when who or what we love is in danger. The danger for me in the 7th grade was that I was not investing in myself. My Father's loving wrath changed my life and made me respect myself, my capacities, and my future. It made my current life possible. In this, he played neither an abusive nor neglectful parent. He expressed love by calling me to work for my well-being.

Walter Brueggemann reminds us that the function of prophetic speech, the tradition of truth-telling in the Hebrew and Christian Scriptures, is to warn us of the consequences of our ways in time to change. Images of God's loving wrath in these Scriptures are an attempt to break through our denial so that we can change our ways. Prophetic speech is neither neglectful nor abusive; it is an act of love.

It took years for me to understand this. The idea and imagery of hell have haunted me. They have often kept loving Christians from engaging in relationships and partnerships with people of diverse wisdom traditions. My Father's refining love is the lens through which I see God's words of warning. But it is very important to remember this: He spoke to me this way very infrequently. The ratio of affirmation to words of accountability was 1,000 to 1. In this, he played neither the abusive nor neglectful parent. He was loving. More loving still is the Creator, who is gracious and abounding in steadfast love, who is compassionate and merciful.

You're My Brother

I attended a PRIDE event in Arlington, Washington. The event had been postponed both due to the threats of White Nationalist groups and the City Council's refusal to obey Washington State law by protecting a permitted event.

I went because, at the time of this writing, Transgender people and the larger LGBTQIA+ communities are the focus of dehumanizing language by White Nationalists. Six months into the year 2023, fourteen Trans people have been violently killed in the United States. Others have died by suicide due to the increasing pressure on them. I feel strongly we are called to show up to support people being dehumanized–even when we don't understand. When a group is being dehumanized, we are responsible for standing up with and behind them.

Three men stood with Bibles in their hands, proclaiming that our LGBTQIA+ neighbors and those of us who supported them were going to burn in hell. Our only choice, they said, was to be converted to their position. I engaged with each of them for between five and fifteen minutes per person. I wanted to learn what made them tick. I wanted to provide some relief to those celebrating and claiming their rights and human dignity. These men seemed haunted by the idea of hell. You could see it in their eyes. I felt grief for them.

Now, it must be said most people who believe in an eternal hell don't act in this kind of bullying way. Life, theology, and people are more complicated than that. I am not trying to dehumanize people who believe in hell.

I realized that for these three men, the concept of hell fostered an exclusive in-group and gave license to dehumanize those outside their group. In a rather intense conversation with one, he said he believed that hell was created by God. He seemed to think that God is a prison warden, the earth is parole, and that after we die, human beings are eternally tormented unless we become Christians. He seemed to see himself as working for God as either a prosecuting attorney or a parole officer. I told him that I believe in accountability but that the outcome of accountability is reconciliation and healing.

At the end of the conversation, I called him "brother."

"You aren't my brother," he said.

"We are fellow human beings," I said, "so we are brothers."

"You are a human being, but that isn't enough," he said. "You are not my brother."

"Well, you don't get to decide who my brother is. I consider you my brother," I said.

This image of God as a prison warden is not new. When ancient Ur, Egypt, and Babylon were at the height of domination (remember that these communities were not always so!), they proposed a world much like this. Obey the rulers and the priests, and you went to the good place. Disobey, and you went to the bad place. When others disobey, we can throw them away in the here and now. The disobedient have already given up their humanity, their fate sealed by their own hand. This made their gods into an accessory to violence, enslavement, and injustice. This image of God creates a universe where exclusive in-grouping, dehumanization, and violence IS THE WAY THE UNIVERSE IS, is the way God has made it.

Many Christians believe that God created a universe that sorts people into an in-group that receives eternal rewards and out-groups that suffer eternal dehumanization through torture. Thus, if God is going to treat some people like this in the future, then exclusive in-grouping, dehumanization, and violence can be enacted now. Many Christians thus reduce "love" to converting people. If people refuse, they have made their choice. It's on them. These Christians interpret stories of Jesus respecting and standing up for people in other traditions not as the core of Jesus' message but rather a strategy for conversion.

In Sunday school, I was taught the same. We were born already out of balance on a slippery slope. The only way to escape hell is to get in on the sacrifice of Jesus. The best we can hope for is to make it to heaven, even if it is marred by the knowledge that others, including those we love, are groaning in torment.

Two Images

This view is not inevitable. In fact, it did not become standard in Western Christianity until the Roman Empire adopted Christianity. As in ancient Ur, Egypt, and Babylon, this prison warden's idea of God encouraged obedient citizens and permission to invade other nations to "save them" for the afterlife while stealing from and killing them in this one.

My colleague Chris Hoke works to encourage churches to support formerly incarcerated people. One day, he said to me, "The resurrection of Jesus is a cosmic prison break." He told me that on his journey of faith, he learned that Eastern Christians had a very different understanding. Let's follow his lead and consider these two images.

The first is the Baptistry in Florence, Italy,[61] which symbolizes the Western view of Jesus' resurrection and the second is the Eastern Orthodox Icon of the Resurrection of Christ.[62]

In this image from the baptistry in Florence, Italy, Christ's two hands are making signs. His right hand is making a "thumbs up" sign. This is a signal that those on his right are going to heaven. His left hand is making a "thumbs down" sign. Those on his left are going to hell. There, they are eternally eaten by Satan, digested, reconstituted, basted, and roasted, only to be eaten again. Death, hell, and Satan are not destroyed but are themselves eternal. Those baptized may get the thumbs up, but they had better obey. Many Christians in the West believe this is the only Biblical view.

Now, let's consider the Icon of the Resurrection of Jesus in the Eastern Orthodox tradition.

Jesus' resurrection takes place in the garden. Beneath him are the gates of hell, broken and made irreparable by his resurrection. The locks and chains that distort and deny the image of God in human beings are loosening, their power terrible but only temporary. Death, depicted by a chained man, is the only thing destroyed. Jesus' hands are reaching out to our first parents who embody all human beings. Jesus is not simply reaching out to them but is taking them on a journey with him into the garden. The resurrection of Jesus overcomes the power of the idea of hell in our lives, the power of evil in the world, and the separation from God after death. The forces of evil and death itself are overcome for all human beings and the created world in the resurrection of Jesus.

This is an even more ancient tradition than the idea of hell in the Baptistry in Florence. This idea from Eastern Christianity is in the Bible, as we will see below. We don't have to believe in forever torture to believe in God or love Jesus.

Take a deep breath and read that again.

Intrinsic Worth

The contradictions inherent in the Western understanding of hell often lead people to reject Christianity, if not Jesus. It often scares Christians out of working with people of other traditions for fear of being excluded with them, socially from others now and from God eternally.

Let's begin with the core issue. Christianity proposes that the Creator has made a moral universe:

- God created human beings as a part of a good and very good creation–with intrinsic worth.
- Because of our intrinsic worth, how we treat each other and the planet matters, therefore humans are held accountable for what we do Ideas of final judgment and various terms, which we translate as "hell," represent this accountability. This encourages us to give thought before we act to harm others. It provides comfort to us when we are hurt that our value will ultimately be honored and that we don't have to undertake retribution. The Creator has "got this."

Based on this God-given intrinsic worth, the Abrahamic traditions offer the Great Commandments to help us understand how to create a more heavenly earth:

- love God more than our tradition or in-group
- love our neighbor as we love ourselves
- steward a thriving ecosystem and an equitable economy

When human beings and human communities fall short of these three teachings, we unleash hell on one another, ourselves, and creation.

The Christian Scriptures include stories of the last judgment. Last judgment stories were used in the Jewish tradition to state and debate the deep values of the Creator. They were an attempt to help people see the way our individual and collective actions have hellish consequences. Jesus was clear in his judgment story (Matthew 25) that what God values is care for one another, especially those who are vulnerable. These stories function to help us assess the extent to which our lives reflect the Great Commandments and to turn around (repent) when our lives do not.

Again, the issue being addressed is the idea of a moral universe based on the intrinsic value of humans and creation.

Certainly, heaven can't be heaven if people are doing harm to each other. Those who have experienced violence don't want unrepentant perpetrators to live next door to them forever. Revelation insists that in the newly re-created earth we will be healed, whole, and safe:

> "People will bring into it the glory and the honor of
> the nations. But nothing unclean will enter it, nor
> anyone who practices abomination or falsehood, but
> only those who are written in the Lamb's book of
> life."
> Revelation 21:26-27

There are three steps to heaven coming to earth in Revelation. First, the domination system personified in Babylon the Great is destroyed. Second, death and Hades, which empower domination systems, are thrown into the lake of fire. They will no longer assail the creation. Humans, animals, and the rest of the created world will be safe from evil and domination. The third step is that people who participate in evil are also put in the lake of fire. This is called the "second death." The question is: Is this lake of fire their permanent situation?

Earlier in Revelation 19, the kings of the nations who participate in the evil of a domination system are killed with the "sword that came from his [the messenger's] mouth." Nobody can hold a sword in their mouth. The sword is a symbol of the truth. But a few short chapters later, the kings of the nations come into the New Jerusalem–into heaven on earth. Barbara Rossing and many other scholars suggest that they have indeed gone through a death, but a baptismal death. They have undergone a God-given transformation. Fire is thus not destruction but purification. Because of this transformation, they can enter the New Jerusalem, whose gates are never closed.

Accountability and transformation are required for human beings. But our need for change does not erase our value in the Creator's eyes. Rossing suggests that those thrown into the lake of fire, which is eternal, are not there forever. Death does not have the last word with Jesus, and the second death does not have the last word with human beings. Rather, it is like a refiner's fire that burns away our capacity for evil. Repentance is always hard, even painful. This is why baptism into Christ was described as a "daily death and resurrection." Baptism isn't easy. The lake of fire is not, I suspect, a metaphor for a comfortable experience. Being confronted with the ways we have harmed each other and the creation is always painful.

The problem is that we often interpret these stories and the book of Revelation through the lens of Dante's Inferno, even though the Inferno is not a part of our Scriptures. Satan is not living it up in an eternal buffet of human beings, as the imagery of the Baptistry suggests. Yet, these writings and this imagery often shape the way we read scripture. Through them, we come to believe not in accountability but in eternal torture.

In history, ancient domination systems used theology to oppress people. Sadly, many powerful leaders in Western Christianity have distorted the Bible to propose a similar system: Disobey the rulers, you end up in a bad place; obey them, and you go to heaven but will forever remember loved ones who are not with you.

But the idea of forever torture does something else to us in the here and now. It undermines the very notion of love of neighbor. The Western Tradition has often been interpreted to say that the universe is basically a sorting mechanism in which God's forever in-group is formed. Those in the in-group are forever rewarded. Those who are a part of the out-group are forever tortured, rejected, and thrown away. This leads people to imagine the humanity of out-groups is already forfeit. Thus, love of neighbor and love of enemy, two core teachings of Jesus, are emptied of their meaning. How can we love enemies into neighbors when God doesn't? As a born-again family member once said to me, "What does it matter if some Iraqis die earlier in the war than they would otherwise? They have already made their eternal decision."

Instead of being called to be a blessing to all, it's every person for themselves and us and God against them.

For many, however, heaven can't be heaven if human beings are being perpetually tortured somewhere else. For me, a universe in which human beings are handed over to eternal torment is not a moral universe at all. For me, a God who throws people away into forever torture is no God at all.

I don't believe this is the message of scripture. Rather, it is the message of domination culture designed to encourage fearful obedience and to divide us from one another by emptying *love of neighbor* of its meaning. The message of scripture is of the intrinsic worth of human beings and the creation and God's work to restore us to this worth.

Bible, Not Bullying

The three men at the PRIDE event suggested their view is "just what the Bible says." One of them told me that if I didn't believe in their understanding of the prison warden God and hell, I would end up in hell myself. This was an attempt to bully me. But quite often in the Bible, warnings about our behavior are directed at those who bully others, not to bully people who are being bullied.

Contrary to this view of a prison warden God, I suggest six important passages of scripture that suggest that God seeks the ultimate restoration of all humans and the re-creation of the world.

First, in Colossians 1:21, Paul says that "in Christ, God is pleased to be reconciled to all things." Paul does not say some things, some people. Paul says, "All things." This passage suggests that all things have been created in Christ and that the nature of the universe is revealed in Jesus' vulnerable love. As all things were created through him, all things will be healed and made whole through him. But this does not mean it is through belief or even knowledge of him. **The Creator's power to heal extends beyond our belief to heal, just as God's power precedes the creation itself.** Those humans called to be a part of Jesus' Kindom are called to participate in this healing and to find our true identity in doing so.

Romans suggests something very similar:

> Therefore, just as one man's trespass led to
> condemnation for all, so one man's act of
> righteousness leads to justification and life for all.
> Romans 5:18

For Paul, the power of the Creator revealed in Jesus extends to all. Christ represents God's desire to heal the whole cosmos.

Second, Jesus calls on his disciples to "love your enemies and do good to those that harm you." (Matthew 6) It begs the question, "Would Jesus call us to do something that God refuses to do?" That makes no sense. Again, "love" does not mean to think well of or have positive feelings about others. Love means to work for the well-being of another. Torture does not create well-being.

In my own struggle with this issue, I have sought to take Jesus at his word. The third verse is Jesus praying from the cross: "Father, forgive them for they know not what they do." He does not say, "Forgive them if they repent, or if they believe the right things, or if they become Christian." He is saying this about and within the hearing of the very people who were torturing him to death and who would likely get up and do it the next day.

For me, the words of Christ from the cross should be used to interpret the judgment stories in the Christian Scriptures, including the ending of the book of Revelation. A moral universe that reaches its fullness in the heaven on Earth envisioned in Revelation cannot be moral unless there is accountability, safety, healing, and a guarantee of peace and justice. A moral universe cannot be moral unless there is ultimate reconciliation between people.

What about Jesus and "hell?" Jesus used the term *gehenna*. This is the garbage dump on the South side of Jerusalem. It used to be the site of child sacrifice, thought to be commanded by the gods in many Middle Eastern religions, including some traditions in the Hebrew tradition. Jesus used this term in a larger tradition of condemning behaviors and calling for accountability. He is not authorizing European, Middle Ages concepts of hell. Jesus also used the term *hades*. Hades is a Greek concept of the dead in a waiting room for judgment. Again, Jesus used a well-known term to encourage accountability for both individuals and as part of a critique of traditions that support domination. In both cases, Jesus uses these terms to promote self and group reflection on how we are living out the Three Great Teachings. Self-reflection and repentance from doing harm are the appropriate responses to the idea of a moral universe.

Many of the early church leaders taught that while hell exists, God rescues people from it.

> "What, therefore, is the scope of Paul's argument in this place [1 Cor. 15:28]? That the nature of evil, at length, be wholly exterminated, and divine, immortal goodness embrace within itself every rational creature; so that of all who were made by God, not one shall be excluded from his Kingdom. All the viciousness that, like corrupt matter, is mingled in things, shall be dissolved and consumed in the furnace of purgatorial fire; and everything that had its origin from God shall be restored to its pristine state of purity."
> Gregory of Nyssa

Paul does not write of hell. But he seems to suggest that all humans, since all have fallen short of love, go through a purifying fire. Here is a fifth important verse:

> For no one can lay any foundation other than the one that has been laid; that foundation is Jesus Christ. Now if anyone builds on the foundation with gold, silver, precious stones, wood, hay, straw— the work of each builder will become visible, for the Day will disclose it, because it will be revealed with fire, and the fire will test what sort of work each has done. If what has been built on the foundation survives, the builder will receive a reward. If the work is burned, the builder will suffer loss; the builder will be saved, but only as through fire.
> 1 Corinthians 3:11-15

The Creator who created us with intrinsic value will respond to us, both when we do harm and when we are harmed, with restoration. This restoration is what the whole idea of the Messiah is about - the new heaven and new earth. Because of the intrinsic value of all creation, God holds us accountable for how we live out the three Great Commandments. The purpose of accountability is not punishment but reconciliation. The builder, that is, people, will be saved even when what they built is not built on the love of God and neighbor.

The question for some is that once we die, are we beyond even the power of God for reconciliation? But this leaves out many parts of scripture, including a sixth important verse from 1 Peter:

> Since, therefore, Christ suffered in the flesh, arm
> yourselves also with the same intention (for
> whoever has suffered in the flesh has finished with
> sin), so as to live for the rest of your earthly life no
> longer by human desires but by the will of God.
> You have already spent enough time doing what the
> Gentiles like to do, living in licentiousness, passions,
> drunkenness, revels, carousing, and lawless idolatry.
> They are surprised that you no longer join them
> in the same excesses of dissipation, and so they
> blaspheme. But they will have to give an account
> to him who stands ready to judge the living and
> the dead. For this is the reason the gospel was
> proclaimed even to the dead so that, though they
> had been judged in the flesh as everyone is judged,
> they might live in the spirit as God does.
> 1 Peter 4:1-6

The passage suggests very clearly that Jesus has proclaimed the gospel "to the dead" so that "they might live in the spirit as God does." Many Christians suggest that at death, our relationship with God is "locked in." This limits God's freedom. This passage suggests no such limit but that God is always free to continue God's work of restoring humans and the creation.

Jesus also used words translated as "eternal torment." But we may be "group-thinking" our way to this translation. The word *aonion* likely means, according to N.T. Wright, not "forever" but rather be speaking of the difference between the eon of domination and the eon of eternity. It is referring to when truth-telling comes, not "how long." Jesus often speaks of "this age" and the "age to come." The word *kolasin* means "correction," not torture.

Some will say that this interpretation will lead people to lawlessness. To them, I say: Many Christian slave traders and enslavers believed in hell. Many who committed genocide of Indigenous people on this continent believed in hell. Did it stop them? No. They said that by enslaving and taking land, they were saving these non-Christians from hell and so justified making their lives hell on earth.

I have come to see that the exact opposite is true. Since ethics begins with the goodness of the creation, to deny this goodness undermines ethics and undermines love.

I am not saying we don't experience hell. I just don't think the God revealed in Jesus would abandon people to it. Hell is not a sufficient response to the hell on earth we often create for one another when we fall short of the Great Commandments. In the Apostles' Creed, Jesus descends to the dead. He breaks the power of hell for all time and in the here and now.

> And I tell you, you are Peter, and on this rock I will
> build my church, and the gates of Hades will not
> prevail against it.
> Matthew 16.18

The church of Jesus has often served as the marketing team for the power of hell rather than living into the power of God to break hell open now and in the age to come.

Reconciling and Healing God

After considering all of this I would add a third statement to the basis of a moral universe:

- God created human beings as a part of a good and very good creation–with intrinsic worth.
- Because of our intrinsic worth, how we treat each other and the planet matters, therefore humans are held accountable for what we do. Ideas of final judgment and various terms, which we translate as "hell," represent this accountability. This encourages us to give thought before we act to harm others. It provides comfort to us when we are hurt that our value will ultimately be honored and that we don't have to undertake retribution. The Creator has "got this."
- When we (all of us) engage in harming others (all of us), we are held accountable for our actions. In this, the intrinsic worth of those we harmed and ourselves is honored. To honor the intrinsic value of all human beings, the goal of accountability is reconciliation, not eternal punishment.

- When we are harmed, we need acknowledgment, restitution, & heartfelt apologies. Then, we can begin to consider forgiveness and reconciliation.
- When we do harm, we need to acknowledge what we did, engage in inner work, make restitution, and receive forgiveness when it is offered.

Eternal punishment denies the intrinsic value of human beings. It implies that the Creator does not love us as we are, or value us, but only values what we do. This is not a love any parent, friend, or married partner would recognize as love. Thus, forever punishment, even for the most terrible crimes, undermines the very basis for a moral universe and severs us from the meaning of love of neighbor in the here and now.

Furthermore, it leads some Christians to assume people in other traditions are less than human because they are judged to be doomed to hell. This functions to dehumanize the other groups and to break down the very moral universe they claim hell supports. This understanding of hell as forever punishment enshrines exclusive in-grouping and ultimate dehumanization and violence toward out-groups as essential to the fabric of the universe.

For further reading, I suggest *Her Gates Will Never Be Shut: Hell, Hope, and the New Jerusalem* by New Testament Professor Bradley Jersak. He offers a view into the complexity of the scripture about this topic. He says that the Bible is a bit ambiguous about hell. I think he's right. I suggest that there are times for humans and human societies when our denial of our harm to each other and the earth is so great that only metaphors of ultimate destruction can shake us up enough to create change. Prophetic speech needs to be dramatic to break through our confirmation bias.

Other traditions also speak of accountability. Our Jewish neighbors generally don't build their theology around hell but use the idea as a part of storytelling as an invitation to self and group reflection. Our Muslim neighbors do believe in hell, but listen to the Prophet Mohammed's words (peace be upon him) that one day hell will be empty, as God is compassionate and merciful. Many traditions around the world include warnings about consequences of harmful actions. Our Upper Skagit friends, in the words of my friend Jay Bowen, teach that as a person makes the journey to God, something happens. The evil we did or participated in dissolves like soot as we ascend to the Creator. The ways we have fallen short of enjoying life, helping people, and not hurting anyone are removed from us and destroyed. This is a similar notion to what I now see as the teachings of Jesus.

Is it possible for human beings to reject this reconciliation? Many Christian theologians suggest that the answer must be "yes" as a part of our creation is the gift of free will. Yet such a choice would be ours and not God's. In every moment, the good news is offered again so we might live in the spirit as God does.

As a child, I was haunted by the idea of forever torture in hell. The three men who came to PRIDE are also haunted and, at the parade sought to haunt the good people there. In my life, Dante's imagery played in my head, increasing my fear and eating away at my trust in God. The Hebrew and Christian Scriptures use various words that we translate as "hell" to warn us about denying with our actions the intrinsic worth of ourselves, others, and the earth. This warning arises from love.

God holds us accountable for the purpose of reconciliation. But the Christian vision goes beyond this. By becoming a human being and suffering on the cross in Jesus, God holds Godself accountable to human beings who experience harm. God knows what that is like. By forgiving us, even from the cross, when we do harm, God moves all of us to reconciliation. In the resurrection of Jesus, God signals a healing and reconciliation that is able to heal and reconcile us in our harming and in our hurts. In a universe of freedom in which we choose to create hell on earth, God responds by experiencing that hell, breaking the gates of hell, and leading us into a renewed heaven on earth.

Taking Us to the Bank

As a freshman, I started on the varsity high school basketball team. The reason why I started was clear. As the custodian, my Dad had the keys to the gym. After working ten hours a day, he would take me to do ball handling, passing, and shooting drills. A freshman starting was a big deal in my hometown. After five games, I began to be full of myself, and it showed on the court. Disagreeing with the referee's call, I threw the ball hard back to the ref. The coach took me out of the game.

That night my Dad asked me to go help him clean the bank. This was a small second job for my Dad. I thought how wonderful it was that I was willing to help my Dad with his little job now that I was a basketball star. After we began our routine of cleaning the bank, my Dad said, "You think you are pretty great, don't you?"

"No," I said. "Well, you do. I could see it on your face on the court tonight. You threw the ball back at the ref. You played selfishly. You pouted on the bench. You think you are pretty important."

I began to weep. He was right.

My Father held up a mirror to my behavior, attitude, and impact on others.

While I vacuumed the floor, I wept. And wept. It was indeed an inferno of pain and self-awareness.

On the way home, as we walked silently, he said to me: "Terry, you are a good person, but you are young. You have a lot of pressure on you right now. Don't be too hard on yourself about what happened. Sometimes, we can't handle things without help. I am only trying to help you."

I could only whisper, "Thanks, Dad."

If the idea of hell and judgment haunts you, consider the flaming, refining, loving, passionate-for-my-future anger of my Dad to help you.

Would the Creator do less?

> Is there anyone among you who, if your child asks
> for bread, will give a stone? Or if the child asks for
> a fish, will give a snake? If you then, who are evil,
> know how to give good gifts to your children, how
> much more will your Father in heaven give good
> things to those who ask him!
> Matthew 7:9-10

I didn't start the next game but played very well. On the bus ride home, the coach asked what happened. I told him the story of "my Dad taking me to the bank." The coach said, "Well, I'll have to ask your Dad to take you to the bank before every game." I said, "Please don't do that." This has become a part of our family's lore. All we have to do is ask, "Do we need to take you to the bank?" and our family members begin to engage in self-reflection. I wonder if hell works in a similar way—a kind of shorthand of prophetic speech for looking at the hellish consequences of individual and collective harms.

The Creator may take us to the bank, but only for the good of everyone. God takes us to the bank now and in the age to come. But the doors of hell are broken, and the gates of heaven never shut. On the way home from the bank, the Creator will say, "I am only trying to help you and all your siblings to see each other as human." We will respond, "Thank you, Creator." And the Creator will wipe away the tears from all our faces.

> On either side of the river is the tree of life with its
> twelve kinds of fruit, producing its fruit each month;
> and the leaves of the tree are for the healing of the
> *mishpachah*.
> Revelation 22:2

The universe is not a prison system. God is not the warden. Christians are not the parole officers.

Rather, the universe is inherently good, and we are called to do our part in the coming of God's Kindom on earth as it is in heaven. In Jesus, Christians are invited to embrace our lives as they are and to honor the dignity of our siblings.

A moral universe cannot be moral unless human beings who fall short of loving God, neighbor, and the creation are ultimately reconciled with God, with those harmed, and restored to the fullness of the image of God. All of us fall short of love. In the power of God, we are invited to live into the fullness of God's image when we, redeemed by the gift of God from hell, from hell on earth, and perhaps even from the idea of hell, participate in the restoration of the earth and receiving and giving blessings with all the *mishpachah* of the world.

I count myself among those who need and long for such restoration.

Chapter Twenty-Eight: Weaving a Story of Hope

Many traditions around the world teach the unity in diversity of the creation and the human family. Many are monotheistic, others polytheistic, and still others do not refer to a god at all.

The Abrahamic tradition teaches that there is one Creator in whom we live, move, and have our being. One Creator invites us to recognize each other as fully human. We have differences in language, culture, wisdom, tradition, and physical characteristics, but we are all children of one Creator. Our creation as a part of the earth's ecosystem is an act of pure gift, complete grace, and boundless generosity. Seeing all of this, the Creator was pleased and said, "Behold, it is good, very good."

We celebrate the unity in diversity of the human family by remembering our common parents. We share almost all our DNA with each other and much of our DNA with our fellow creatures. We are not just symbolically part of one family. We are quite literally part of one another.

Human beings are mortal. We need food, shelter, sleep, safety, meaning, and community to survive and thrive. We all share some vulnerabilities. We can reject life as it is and seek to be God and to dominate one another and the planet of which we are a part. When we act this out, we cause ourselves, one another, and the earth great pain. We do this when we arrange ourselves into status-keeping systems and engage in exclusive in-grouping, dehumanization, and violence towards each other. We do this when we exploit the earth instead of stewarding it, both for future generations and for the creation's own good, very good life. Instead of the mutuality God envisions, we fall into line with domination, seeking power over each other.

God called Abraham to start a tradition and a family. This family would be blessed: that is, God would both speak well of them and work for their well-being. This blessing was a subset of a larger value that the Creator holds dear: the blessing of all the *mishpachah* of the world. The blessing of all the families, nations, tribes, cultures, and religions of the world. The calling of Abraham's family was to be a blessing to all the *mishpachah* of the world.

Liberation from Egypt

For a time, the people of Egypt used God's language to bless an unjust system. They enslaved human beings. God does not consent to be used to bless such systems. The Creator called Moses to leave his shepherding fields and lead the People of Israel out of Egypt, out of the house of slavery. God takes the side of oppressed and marginalized beings to shake apart unjust systems in the hope for us to return to a mutual way of life.

This mutual way of life is complicated. While human beings do cooperate with one another, we also have competing interests. To honor this complexity, the Abrahamic tradition teaches Three Great Teachings that hold good and very good things in tension with each other

- love God more than our in-group or tradition
- love our neighbor as we love ourselves
- steward a thriving ecosystem and a just economy

Any way we might live out these core teachings is always secondary to the Creator. No matter how sure we may be that our way is right, only God is ultimate. God continues to teach, and we are to remain open to learning, growing, and loving more deeply.

Jesus and the Kindom of God

Jesus of Nazareth heard God's call to lead within this larger Abrahamic tradition. The Roman Empire had imposed a kingdom of domination: taking land, exploiting human beings, and lording it over others. Their rule created a crisis. How might people formed by the story of freedom from both Egypt and Babylon respond to the overwhelming power and seductiveness of the Roman occupation? From the time he would sit on his mother's lap, Jesus learned about the meaning of monotheism, the call of Abraham and the God who desires the well-being of all cultures and traditions, and God's freeing of the People of Israel.

It's vital to say, at this point, that he was not the only Jewish person to act faithfully to the Abrahamic tradition within that context. In response, he proclaimed the Kindom of God. This Kindom was near. He called people to stop conforming to the kingdom of domination and to make a new beginning. He called people to trust that something new could come. He taught that they could begin to live into the vision of God's Kindom even during the Roman Empire. The vision could be seen as they would share food and clothing. He called people to live out a deep wisdom: that even if we saw each other as enemies before, our hearts will change when we do good for and with each other. When social cohesion is low, we can alternatively eat together, honor one another in public, and work for the common good together. Jesus called for a conversion from living the values of a culture of domination to one of mutuality, where we hold **power with** instead of **power over each other.**

He debated with a Syrophoenician woman, healed a centurion's servant, and told a positive story about a Samaritan. Within a domination culture, Jesus worked to create a community of partnership and mutuality, saying, "it shall not be so among you." He washed the feet of his disciples, giving up his status, and said we should wash one another's feet. He accepted a woman to be an official disciple and prepared her for her own public leadership.

The Romans knew that Jesus' way of love was a threat. Domination only survives by dividing. So, they did to him what they did on an industrial scale: they crucified him. This instrument of political terror kept many in fear. But God raised him from the dead to empty the cross and all forms of terror of their power. Love wins. Life wins. Jesus changed the game for these disciples, who, in turn, began to risk themselves for the vision of the Kindom of God. Jesus' resurrection offered greater freedom for disciples to love their neighbor.

They welcomed people of all in-groups into their community (Matthew 28:18-20) while recognizing that people of other traditions who loved the Creator and their neighbor were accepted by God (Acts 10:34-35 and Romans 2:14-16).

They told a story about how the Kingdom of Rome, and domination culture in general, symbolized as Babylon the Great, would end, saying, "God will create a new heaven and a new earth." The kings of the earth who served Babylon the Great would weep at her downfall. But then, seemingly changed in a baptismal process, enter the new Jerusalem. A tree is there on both sides of the river for the healing of the nations. God will wipe the tears from all our faces, and we will live as God intends.

We are sent, as Jesus was sent, to participate in the healing and continued creation of the earth and to be a blessing to all the *mishpachah* of the world.

Blessing Forgotten

Even the first disciples did not escape the dangers of our common human vulnerability. In the earliest Christian writings, there were seeds of exclusive in-grouping that would metastasize into Antisemitism, racism, and violence throughout history and in our own time. Separated from the Jewish context of the 1st century and the deep tradition of the Hebrew Scriptures, they began to distort very basic, important words like sacrifice and salvation and neighbor.

Christianity was taken over by the very empire that crucified Jesus. The Nicaean Creed says that Pontius Pilate crucified Jesus. This is a lie–by–omission. It obscures the truth that the death of Jesus was the outcome of Roman policy. It doesn't take much to change a wisdom tradition. Change the meaning of a few words, and you change the whole thing. Change love from "risking for the community's well-being" to "converting people." Turn salvation from "the healing of the whole creation" to a "get into heaven card." Turn sacrifice from "a spiritual practice" into the idea that "God needs payment to forgive." Change these and you have a religion that can be used for anything.

Later, during the Crusades, Christian rulers sent soldiers to kill Muslims and Jews as enemies of Christ–ignoring what Jesus actually said about enemies. The Doctrines of Discovery blessed exclusive in-grouping, dehumanization, and violence through theft of land, enslavement, and genocide. Christians moved to this continent, downloading exclusive in-grouping, dehumanization, and violence into our theology, practice, poetry, worship, and who we hang out with.

It was taught that God wanted it this way. That God would be angry if we disagreed. We were told that God needed violence and blood to forgive–that violence and authoritarianism were baked into the cake of the world, and we must eat it.

Threads

Even so, people of every age worked to remember how Jesus faithfully responded to the occupation of the Roman Empire from the wisdom of the Abrahamic tradition.

A bishop in Egypt returned to the city to serve those impacted by an epidemic. Desert Fathers kept a vision alive in their poetry and silence. Francis gave up power over others to serve with others, recognizing his common heritage with the Sultan. Julian of Norwich lifted up a vision in which all will be well, and all manner of things will be well. The Eastern tradition kept alive a whole different notion of the power of Jesus' resurrection. Reformers in every age returned to the texts to find what was lost and to repair that which was broken. Black pastors and church members gathered in church basements to strengthen human rights for all, knowing the violence that White Nationalists and avowed supremacists would inflict upon them. Many Christians gathered at Standing Rock to stand behind the Indigenous tribes in their struggle for treaties to be honored.

Movements based on the story of Jesus lifted up another way to live. The children of formerly enslaved people and the children of former enslavers began to see each other differently. In the lives and leadership of African American churches, leaders, and theologians, Christians caught a glimpse of Jesus as a public, nonviolent leader.

Some churches began to find mutual humanity with Indigenous siblings. Some began to respect the ancient wisdom of Indigenous tradition, to repent of boarding schools, to weep at the genocide of fellow human beings, and to build a future together.

Blessing to All the In-groups

Human beings are being dis-membered from one another, but God is re-membering us to one another.

To take our own part in this, Christians are remembering the meaning of one Creator, one set of original parents, and the pluralistic call of Abraham to be a blessing to all the mishpachah of the earth. Christians are remembering Jesus' vision of the Kindom of God and how God seeks to disrupt unjust systems and societies so that we can live in partnership, honoring and respecting each other. Christians are learning to tell an Origin Story in a way

that respects God's promises to and throug⌐
bors. We have so often taught and preached aⅠ
forms much of the basis for the White Nationⅰ
continues to poison our nation. Christians are Ⅰ
the Mysterious Supreme One and not take ourseⅠ
Christians are learning to understand that Jesus sacⅠ⌐
to lift the veil of fear and that his followers are called ⌐
same. Christians are learning that a core part of the ChristianⅠ.
is to honor, respect, and embrace the full humanity of people of aⅠ
wisdom traditions. Christians are learning that the vision of the
early Church was to heal the earth and to recognize the unity in
diversity of all the mishpachah of the world.

In this work, we are equals. The Creator gives us different gifts
but values all of us the same. The person who speaks is no more or
less important, honored, and valuable. The person who makes the
coffee is every bit as much a part of this blessing as the one who
speaks.

I was raised in a culture and a church based on exclusive in-
grouping, dehumanization, and violence toward people in other
in-groups. I am still and will always be in recovery from this. But
every step I take along this path not only reunites me with others
and the creation. It restores me to myself and the Creator.

Many Christians are working hard to recover from Christian
supremacy. Many are working hard to recover from White supremacy. In walking this path of repentance, we are being faithful
to Jesus. With each painful realization comes the joy of new life for
ourselves and new life with our fellow human beings.

Christians are called to continue to recognize a baptismal identity: that all the families of the earth are beloved. Experiencing this
love through Jesus Christ, Christians are welcoming the disorientation from domination and being reoriented to the Kindom of God.

Further, Christians are called to act and to stop being so passive.

Another Lutheran pastor once said to me, "You really love works,
don't you?" He was referencing a commonly held distortion of
Martin Luther's teaching. Luther taught that we are justified by
grace, by faith apart from "works of law," quoting Paul. Lutherans
and other Christian traditions often use theology to justify passivity. He was arguing that working for the common good is unfaithful. I responded sarcastically, "Yes, Abraham was asked to go on
a journey, and he said, 'No because doing so would be a work.'

Moses was asked to free God's people, and Moses said, 'No because doing so would be a work.' And God asked Mary if she would bear Jesus, and Mary said, "No because doing so would be a work.' What you seem to be saying is that responding to God's call to love our neighbor or work for the common good is to sin. I reject that. Responding to God's call does not reject God's love for us. It is a response to it."

To his credit, he took a deep breath and recognized that something in his theology and actions needed to change. I respect that.

To people on the street who are angry at Christian theology and to Christians seeking to justify themselves by arguing about theology, I often say, "I don't care what you believe. If your tradition teaches you to stand with your neighbor when they need you, to bring healing to the ecosystem, and to work for the common good, then let's work together."

While theology and practice really matter, they only matter to the degree that they lead us to embody, as Jesus did, the Three Great Teachings—even while knowing that we will always fall short of them. Again, this doesn't deny the Creator's love for all but rather honors the Creator's image in us.

Human beings are being torn apart. Human beings are vulnerable. Humans are always tempted to reject life as it is and slide toward dominance and submission, exclusive in-groups, dehumanization, and violence. The internet slander machine is amplifying all that dehumanizes. AI will likely soon flood the zone with disinformation obscuring what is real and leaving humans not knowing how to act and who to trust. Political groups work hard to divide people. News media organizations can choose to share only negative stories and perspectives.

But all wisdom traditions offer insight and plans of action to move forward together to honor our Creator, to honor the unity of life.

When we grow to know each other, we do good with and for each other. When we stand together in public and honor one another's humanity, we can take part in God's re-membering of the human family.

Our Choice

In response to the inequity of our day, we can stand with communities experiencing marginalization. We can ally by standing behind, creating space for, and publicly associating with those being dehumanized–as Jesus did. We can learn to welcome reputational harm from "eating with sinners" as a blessing.

In response to the division of our day, we can gather with people of diverse wisdom, traditions, cultures, and political ideologies to know each other, work for the common good, and respect each other in public. We can build social trust with each other.

Adding more pressure to what divides us, the climate crisis will lead to increased tensions through diminishing resources, increasing climate refugees, and anxiety about the future. The climate crisis will increase the power of exclusive in-grouping and dehumanization through these tensions, cross-cultural interactions, and fear. In response, we can live out the core values of the Abrahamic tradition and stand together with those of diverse traditions and cultures to address these challenges.

In every neighborhood, in every small town, in every city and suburb, communities of wisdom have the power to go together into a brighter future. We know how to do potlucks. Let's unleash the power of the potluck! We know how to work together for the common good through service projects. Let's do it. We know how to march in a parade or to create a solidarity event. Let's do it.

So many of us long for something we can do to mend the dangerous state of our social cohesion, and we often wish for a switch that can fix it all at once. Jesus rejected this temptation when he refused to sit on the imperial throne. While there is no one switch, we can do much together. The hate groups seek to shut us down, to make us afraid and passive. But there are so many more Americans who want to live in a peaceful and just community. They need the leadership of communities of wisdom to form public partnerships of mutual respect. Our silence contributes to their despair. Our collective work will lead to hopeful, joyous action waiting to be unleashed.

Jesus announced the Kindom of God and then he helped people to see how they could begin to live toward it in their everyday life. One person, one family, one city at a time, people began to be restored to one another. They grew from competition to cooperation. They grew from enemies to friends. In doing so, they honored not only the image of God in others but in themselves. In finding each other, they found themselves in the one Creator, lover of souls, and healer of the universe. We can, too.

It is not too late, even if it feels that way.

Through the ages and among us today are those who kept the faith in dire circumstances, who sat in the shadows of slavery and genocide and did not give up. As a Christian, I believe that God joins people in those shadowy places, and there, the light of God's Kindom shines.

I no longer believe the Christian tradition teaches that it is merely permissible to work with people of diverse cultures. I have come to believe that **knowing, respecting, and working with people of diverse traditions is an inherent part of being faithful to Jesus.**

When the religious leader asked Jesus, "Who is my neighbor?" he was really asking, "Who can I exclude?" Human beings are vulnerable to exclusive in-grouping: Christians, perhaps foremost. We easily dehumanize others. Dehumanization leads to violence. All of these can gain momentum and power when there is scarcity, as will increasingly be the case with climate change.

Jesus' response to the religious leader was to tell a positive story about a dehumanized group. Jesus ate with, stood with, and enjoyed the company of people of many wisdom traditions and cultures. As a leader in the Abrahamic tradition, Jesus embodied one Creator, the call of Abraham to be a blessing to all the *mishpachah*, his vision for the Kindom of God, and the ultimate healing of the tribes of the world in a restored earth. He was so committed to the Creator's vision that he risked his life for it. He took up his cross in the hope that others would be freed from Roman state-sponsored terror and the despair that nothing could change.

For Christians, his resurrection means that the gates of fear, death, hell, and despair are broken open, and the gates of the New Earth are never shut. In the hope for the new creation, we offer our lives in service for its fulfillment.

> I consider that the sufferings of this present time
> are not worth comparing with the glory about to
> be revealed to us. For the creation waits with eager
> longing for the revealing of the children of God; for
> the creation was subjected to futility, not of its own
> will but by the will of the one who subjected it, in
> hope that the creation itself will be set free from
> its bondage to decay and will obtain the freedom
> of the glory of the children of God. We know that
> the whole creation has been groaning in labor
> pains until now; and not only the creation, but we

> ourselves, who have the first fruits of the Spirit,
> groan inwardly while we wait for adoption, the
> redemption of our bodies.
> Romans 8:18-23

I was born into White Christian Supremacy. But I was not born for it. You weren't either. The Creator has more beautiful ways for us to live and is restoring what was taken from us. Jesus invites his followers to take the long, painful, joyous, and healing journey of daily baptism to find our identity among all the Creator's children, all made in God's image.

We must make a choice.

We will stand together as human beings or we will fall apart. We can retreat into our little in-groups. We can take all the firewood for ourselves, warm and fearful while the world burns. Or we can hear once again the call of the Creator to recognize and honor the dignity of every *mishpachah*, to risk ourselves for our common good, and find ourselves a part of God's beautiful, diverse creation. We can sit in silent passivity. Or we can do our small part in the healing and creation of the world, find deep meaning in doing our part, and find our common humanity among all our siblings. Jesus invites us to go and do likewise.

It is time to get going.

Let's go together!

Section Six Bible Studies

Jesus Honoring Our Common Humanity

Acts 2:42-47

Awe came upon everyone, because many wonders and signs were being done by the apostles. All who believed were together and had all things in common; they would sell their possessions and goods and distribute the proceeds to all, as any had need. Day by day, as they spent much time together in the temple, they broke bread at home and ate their food with glad and generous hearts, praising God and having the goodwill of all the people. And day by day the Lord added to their number those who were being saved.

Reflection

The people in the community of Jesus were being saved. Saved means being healed from the culture of Roman domination to the Kindom of God. They ate food with glad and generous hearts and shared what they had for the needs of each. Instead of competing for status, they found their unity in diversity as holy children of the Holy One. Instead of stealing from each other, they shared. The Kindom of God is grace and love lived out in everyday life.

Instead of creating an exclusive in-group, they continued to grow a community dedicated to seeing the humanity of each person and the value of every group.

They created a new in-group, which was open to people of all cultures. Participating in the Kindom of God in real life is called salvation.

Jesus calls us to do the same and, with glad and generous hearts, praise God for the blessing of embodying, if only imperfectly, God's Kindom come on earth as it is in heaven.

Hey, What About This Verse?

2 Corinthians 6:14

Do not be mismatched with unbelievers. For what partnership is there between righteousness and lawlessness? Or what fellowship is there between light and darkness?

Reflection

This passage is typically interpreted to mean that Christians should not respect, relate to, or work with people of other wisdom traditions. To better understand the text, remember that Jesus preached the Kindom of God in the domination culture of the Roman Empire. The Kindom of God was emerging within the Kingdom of Rome. Paul suggested that Christians living out the values of the Kindom need to be careful not to marry people or partner with people committed to the values of the Kingdom of Rome. It's like a person who works for racial equity marrying a member of the KKK.

Christians work with Christ to engage the larger culture because Jesus engaged in public leadership. The message of 2 Corinthians honors the hard reality of living out a value system of love, justice, and respect for all humans in an unjust system. We need an adequate support system from our family, friends, and church to engage in public leadership. Jesus himself sought support from God, his larger group of disciples, and his inner strength by taking time to rest and refresh himself.

Some people use this text to imply that Christians should isolate themselves, but this is not what it says. Paul calls us to live out a ministry of reconciliation for people divided from and harming each other. We are called to be "in but not of" a culture of domination and seek its healing.

Jesus resisted his disciples' assumption that they were part of an exclusive in-group by reminding them that "Whoever is not against us is for us" (Mark 9:40). In 1 Corinthians, Paul writes that Christians should not spend their energy judging people of other traditions because only God knows the full truth of anyone or any tradition (1 Cor 5:12-13). Further, in Acts 10, we see how God helps Peter begin to understand that people in other traditions love God and do what is right.

This text is not suggesting that Christians cannot work with people of other traditions, rather, that we should not look for support from people committed to or captivated by a Domination culture. It follows, then, that if we find people of other traditions that have values similar to the Kindom of God, we could know, respect, and work with them. In faithfulness to Jesus, a leader in the Abrahamic tradition, we are not called to wall ourselves off from others. Rather, we are called to be a blessing to all tribes, clans, cultures, and traditions and offer our best with humility and find that they will have blessings for us too.

Download Discussion Questions, Action Steps, & Resources:

https://pathstounderstanding.org/gdl/

If you would like Let's Go Together in your community,
contact us at together@pathstounderstanding.org

Learn more on our YouTube channel:
https://www.youtube.com/@pathstounderstanding9918

Join us for on-demand and live courses at the Paths Network:
https://www.pathsnetwork.org

Endnotes

[1] Bruce Malina and Richard Rorhbaugh, Social-Science Commentary on the Synoptic Gospels: Second Edition, Fortress Press, Minneapolis, 2003, Pg. 271

[2] Bruce Malina and Richard Rorhbaugh, Social-Science Commentary on the Synoptic Gospels: Second Edition, Fortress Press, Minneapolis, 2003

[3] https://www.prri.org/research/competing-visions-of-america-an-evolving-identity-or-a-culture-under-attack/

[4] Robert Pape, https://news.uchicago.edu/story/insurrectionist-movement-us-larger-and-more-dangerous-expected-research-finds

[5] https://www.prri.org/research/competing-visions-of-america-an-evolving-identity-or-a-culture-under-attack/

[6] https://psycnet.apa.org/buy/1997-04812-006

[7] https://www.huffpost.com/entry/is-religion-the-cause-of-_b_1400766 and http://news.bbc.co.uk/2/hi/programmes/wtwtgod/3513709.stm

[8] University of Hawaii, https://www.hawaii.edu/powerkills/MURDER.HTML

[9] Sallie McFague, Life Abundant: Rethinking Theology and Economy for a Planet in Peril, Fortress Press, Minneapolis, 2001, Pg. 81

[10] The Study Quran: A New Translation and Commentary, Seyyed Hossein Nasr, Ed. Harper One, New York, 2015

[11] https://youtu.be/8SJi0sHrEI4 A New Understanding of Human History and the Roots of Inequality | David Wengrow | TED

[12] https://youtu.be/MiC-fnLgfls

[13] N.T. Wright, Paul for Everyone, Westminster, John Knox Press, Louisville, Pg. 98-99

[14] Walter Brueggemann, Genesis, Interpretation: A Bible Commentary for Teaching and Preaching, James Luther

Mays, Ed. John Knox Press, Atlanta, Pg. 120

[15] Walter Brueggemann, Genesis, Interpretation: A Bible Commentary for Teaching and Preaching, James Luther Mays, Ed. John Knox Press, Atlanta, Pg. 119

[16] Joan Goodnick Westenholz (1996), "Ur – Capital of Sumer", Royal Cities of the Biblical World, Jerusalem: Bible Lands Museum

[17] We especially like the Interfaith Peacemaking Teams of by Omnia Institute for Contextual Leadership: https://www.omnialeadership.org/

[18] https://www.prri.org/research/competing-visions-of-america-an-evolving-identity-or-a-culture-under-attack/

[19] R. J. Rummel, Statistics of Democide: Genocide and Mass Murder since 1900 (Charlottesville, VA: Center for National Security Law, School of Law, University of Virginia, 1997; and Transaction Publishers, Rutgers University), http://www.hawaii.edu/powerkills/notes5.htm

[20] https://founders.archives.gov/?q=religion%20Author%3A%22Adams%2C%20Abigail%22&s=1111312121&r=41&sr=

[21] https://www.smithsonianmag.com/smithsonian-institution/why-thomas-jefferson-owned-qur-1-180967997/

[22] https://rootandbranches.org/wp-content/uploads/2012/03/eck_what_is_pluralism_2.pdf

[23] Jaroslav Pelikan, The Christian Tradition: A History of the Development of Doctrine (Alternate title: The Emergence of the Catholic Tradition) (Chicago: University of Chicago Press, 1971) 222

[24] Carol Schersten LaHurd Darrell Jodock Kathryn Mary Lohre, Engaging Others, Knowing Ourselves: A Lutheran Calling in a Multi-Religious World, Lutheran University Press, Minneapolis, 2016

[25] Isabel Wilkerson, Caste: The Origin of Our Discontents, Random House, NY, 2020

[26] Caste systems are comprised of eight pillars: • Divine Will – the system is "just the way it is" and "the will of God" • Heritability – social status is acquired at birth • Endogamy – no marriage between castes • Purity and Pollution – dominant caste is pure, while others are on a scale of impurity • Occupational Hierarchy – better jobs for the "better people" • Dehumanization and Stigma – denial of the full humanity of people in lower castes • Inherent Superiority and Inferiority – belief that some people are just superior and work harder

[27] This hymn ends with "every knee shall bow." Many assume this means that other wisdom traditions will be conquered by Christ, as if they are invalid. I would argue that the reason every knee can bow to Jesus is that he does not seek power over anyone, does not compete with anyone. Further, this hymn is trying to say that the character of Jesus, is reflective of the true character of God. The very competition and search for supremacy that people bring into this text is unfaithful to the character of God revealed in Jesus

[28] The Christian Tradition: A History of the Development of Doctrine: The Emergence of the Catholic Tradition, Page 12

[29] The Rise of Christianity: How the Obscure, Marginal Jesus Movement Became the Dominant Religious Force in the Western World in a Few Centuries, Rodney Stark, Harper Collins San Fransisco, 1997

[30] Dana C. Munro, "Urban and the Crusaders", Translations and Reprints from the Original Sources of European History, Vol 1:2, (Philadelphia: University of Pennsylvania, 1895), 5-8

[31] Indigenous Values Initiative, "What is the Doctrine of Discovery?," Doctrine of Discovery Project (30 July 2018), https://doctrineofdiscovery.org/what-is-the-doctrine-of-discovery/

[32] Pagans in the Promised Land: Decoding the Doctrine of Discovery, Steven Newcomb, Chicago Review Press, Chicago, 2008

[33] For millennia, many Indigenous people have referred to North America as Turtle Island.

[34] https://doctrineofdiscovery.org/what-is-the-doctrine-of-discovery/

[35] Bruce Malina and Richard Rohrbaugh, Social Science Commentary on the New Testament, Fortress Press, Minneapolis, Pg. 141

[36] Marcus Borg and Dominic Crossan: The Last Week: What the Gospels Really Teach about Jesus' Final Days in Jerusalem (New York: HarperOne, 2007

[37] N.T. Wright, The New Testament and the People of God (San Francisco: Harper Sanfrancisco, 1992) 244-33[8]

[38] Excerpt From, Uncivil Agreement, Lilliana Mason https://books.apple.com/us/book/uncivil-agreement/id1371645449

[39] The use of the word "flesh" here is not a reference to bodies, but rather to the domination culture of the Roman empire. The word "world" likewise is a reference not to the earth and its creatures (including humans) but to the culture the

Romans imposed. For more on this see: Walter Wink, Engaging the Powers, Fortress Press, Minneapolis, 1992, Pg. 61
[40] David Brockman and Ruben Habito, Gospel Among Religions, Orbis, New York, Pg. 50
[41] Sallie McFague, Life Abundant: Rethinking Theology and Economy for a Planet in Peril, Fortress Press, Minneapolis, 2001, Pg. 209
[42] https://www.egyptconnection.com/42-laws-of-maat/
[43] The words "until all is accomplished" has been used in supersessionism. But I think this definition of "all" is too narrow. I think "all" for Jesus is the emergence of the Kindom of God on earth
[44] Copyright © 1974, 2002 Mission Hills Music; www.ButterflySong.com All rights reserved. (BMI) International copyright secured. CCLI - 35445
[45] See more of this interview: https://youtu.be/mm K2PrCZHLc?si=7NDIsnm6SbkDgXhD. Check out more of Devin's work at https://www.irehr.org/
[46] https://news.gallup.com/poll/6367/Most-Segregated-Hour.aspx
[47] Ervin Staub, The Roots of Goodness and Resistance to Evil: Inclusive Caring, Moral Courage, Altruism Born of Suffering, Active Bystandership, and Heroism, Oxford University Press, 2015
[48] Cynthia D. Moe-Lobeda, Resisting Structural Evil, Fortress Press, Minneapolis, 2013
[49] Mary J. Streufert, Ed, Transformative Lutheran Theologies: Feminist, Womanist, and Mujerista Perspectives, Fortress Press, Minneapolis, 2010
[50] Luther, Martin: Pelikan, Jaroslav Jan (Hrsg.); Oswald, Hilton C. (Hrsg.); Lehmann, Helmut T. (Hrsg.): Luther's Works, Vol. 31: Career of the Reformer I. Philadelphia: Fortress Press, 1999, c1957 (Luther's Works 31), S. 31:55
[51] https://buddho.org/buddhism-and-morality-the-five-precepts/#af-te-zien-van-verkeerd-spreken
[52] Challenge 2.0 Episode on the Rohingya: https://youtu.be/hO46MD363-g
[53] https://www.lionsroar.com/commentary-we-must-address-religious-nationalism-to-prevent-buddhism-from-being-perverted-into-a-force-for-evil/
[54] For more on the dehumanization of Muslims, see our animated video: https://youtu.be/PJ1oL6HHQvE
[55] http://scholarcommons.usf.edu/gsp/vol9/iss3/8

56 The Chaos Machine, Max Fisher, Little and
    Brown Company, New York, 2022
57 Christopher Browning, Ordinary Men (New
    York: Harper Perennial, 1992) 184
58 The Study Quran: A New Translation and Commentary,
    Seyyed Nossein Nasr, ED., Harper One, New York, Pg. 1165
59 https://www.smithsonianmag.com/history/gobekli-
    tepe-the-worlds-first-temple-83613665
60 The Rapture Exposed, Barbara Ross-
    ing, Westview Press, 2004, Pg. 35
61 Creative Commons Zero, Public Domain Dedi-
    cation [File:Christ in majesty florence baptistry.
    jpg|Christ_in_majesty_florence_baptistry]
62 Jess Stubbenbord, 2018, Creative Commons Uni-
    versal Public Domain, https://commons.wikimedia.
    org/wiki/File:Istanbul_114_(40761754722).jpg   /

About the Author

The Rev. Terry Kyllo believes that when we forget how to recognize other humans we lose a connection to part of our own humanity. Terry believes we do not have to live this way.

Terry is a Lutheran pastor serving as the executive director of Paths to Understanding (formerly the Treacy Levine Center). Terry started Neighbors in Faith in 2015 to counter anti-Muslim bigotry. Neighbors in Faith is now a program of the Paths to Understanding.

Paths to Understanding bridges bias and builds unity through multifaith peacemaking–people of all wisdom traditions united for the common good.

A graduate of the Lutheran School of Theology at Chicago, he has been a pastor since 1991 and has served in partnership between Episcopalians and Lutherans since 2004.

He is the author of two books, Being Human and Apprenticeship. He was published by the Aspen Institute in their 2018 Pluralism in Peril Report. He has been interviewed by Crosscut.com, KOMO TV, KOMO Radio, TriCity Herald, and appeared on the Challenge 2.0 TV Show.

Terry was the recipient of the Faith Action Network Interfaith Leadership Award in 2016, the Interfaith Leadership Award from the Muslim Association of Puget Sound in 2017, the Sultan and Saint Peace award in 2017 and the Muslim Association of Puget Sound 2018 "Inbound Good" award for a non-Muslim who benefitted the Muslim Community, and the Called to Lead Award in 2018 from the Lutheran School of Theology at Chicago.